THE COMMON GOOD

Social Welfare and the American Future

*Policy Recommendations
of the Executive Panel*

Ford Foundation

Project on

Social Welfare

and the

American Future

Ford Foundation, New York, N.Y.

Library of Congress Cataloging-in-Publication Data

Ford Foundation. Project on Social Welfare and the
    American Future. Executive Panel.
    The common good.
    Bibliography: p.
    1. Public welfare—United States. 2. United States—
Social policy. I. Title.
HV95.F58 1989   361.6'0973   89-7646
ISBN 0-916584-38-0

473   May 1989
© 1989 Ford Foundation

Contents

Foreword

On Aug. 14, 1935, President Franklin D. Roosevelt signed the Social Security Act, historic legislation establishing Federal programs to provide old-age pensions, unemployment insurance, and aid to dependent children. To this day, these programs have constituted the core of the U.S. social welfare system. Much more than the sum of its parts, the Social Security Act of 1935 signaled official recognition of the Federal government's role in providing protection for Americans of all ages and, as President Roosevelt said, represented the "cornerstone in a structure which is being built but is by no means complete."

Over the years that cornerstone proved quite sturdy, remaining largely intact as such measures as health and disability insurance, food and nutritional services, and youth education and training programs were added to the system. Repeatedly, the American public has indicated the high value it ascribes to these programs, even in times of fiscal retrenchment. In recent years, however, new challenges have appeared, leading an increasing number of observers to ask whether the system needs refinement and rethinking.

Increasing global economic competition, changes in family structure, an aging population, and other developments have created new vulnerabilities for Americans and their families. Gaps in health insurance coverage, the lack of coordinated skill-development efforts to meet the needs of a changing work force, and the high cost of long-term care suggest the need to review the appropriateness of our social welfare system. Can it, as currently structured, be made more responsive to these and other needs, or is more fundamental change required to meet the social welfare challenges of the twenty-first century?

This is the question the Foundation set out to address in 1985 when it established the Project on Social Welfare and the American Future. The project was a special initiative that drew on, but remained independent of, the Foundation's regular programs. The project consisted of interlocking components of research, policy analysis, and deliberations by an eleven-member executive panel of citizens representing the business, academic, labor, civic, and civil rights communities.

The panel was chaired by Irving S. Shapiro (former member of the Foundation's Board of Trustees and former Chief Executive Officer of the duPont Company). Other members of the panel were Sol Chaikin (President Emeritus, International Ladies Garment Workers Union); James R. Ellis (Preston, Thorgrimson, Ellis & Holman); Robert F. Erburu (Chairman and Chief Executive Officer, Times Mirror Company); John H. Filer (Tyler Cooper & Alcorn); Hanna H. Gray (President, University of Chicago); Albert O. Hirschman (Professor of Social Sciences, Institute for Advanced Study); Vernon E. Jordan, Jr. (Akin, Gump, Strauss, Hauer & Feld); Eleanor Holmes Norton (Professor of Law, Georgetown University Law Center); Henry B. Schacht (Chairman and Chief Executive Officer, Cummins Engine Company, Inc.); and Mitchell Sviridoff (Director, Community Development Research Center).

In meetings held regularly throughout the course of the project, panel members undertook a careful review of needs and options in such policy areas as Social Security, health care, employment, and poverty. They also maintained a continuing dialogue about the broader goals and values that guide our social welfare choices. *The Common Good: Social Welfare and the American Future* is the report of the executive panel's findings and recommendations.

Panelists were assisted in their deliberations by briefings and commentary from leading social policy experts. Prof. Charles V. Hamilton of Columbia University directed the project's staff, which included assistant director Alice O'Connor, project associates Austin Cooper, Deborah McCoy, and Elena Pell, and staff consultants Leslie Dunbar and Mitchell Ginsberg.

Three outside consultants consistently provided expertise and guidance to staff and panel deliberations: economist Jack Meyer, president of the Washington-based research organization New Directions for Policy; political scientist Hugh Heclo of George Mason University; and Robert D. Reischauer of the Brookings Institution, who was recently appointed director of the Congressional Budget Office. The panel's report was drafted by Jack Meyer in collaboration with Hugh Heclo.

An interdisciplinary research advisory committee, chaired by Heclo, helped to shape questions related to the long-range future of the social welfare system. In addition, the Foundation supported twenty-eight independent research projects (see Appendix B), which will be of longstanding value in efforts to shape policy in years to come. The project also sought out the views and social policy priorities of those who have direct experience with the system—whether as expert policy analysts, program administrators, or members of the general public—in discussion sessions held around the country. These research and policy activities proved helpful in the preparation of reports and briefing materials for panel sessions on specific topics such as health and long-term care, the interrelated causes of and responses to poverty, and the role of the private sector in providing for social welfare. Believing that these unusually comprehensive reports would be of value to a wider audience, the Foundation has published several of them in a series of occasional papers (see Appendix C).

The Foundation funded the project with the expectation that the panel's report would present important policy recommendations for public debate. We are pleased with the panel's final product and hope it will receive serious attention and support.

Franklin A. Thomas
President
Ford Foundation

Chapter One

Social welfare policy in the United States must be fundamentally reformed and modernized. Economic, demographic, and social conditions have changed, but our social policies have not adapted to these changes.

This report considers the social welfare system as a whole. It is fundamentally different from the reports that deal with individual topics like education, welfare, nutrition, or health care. They are separate reviews of the fragmented pieces of our social welfare system; this is an effort to transcend its splintered segments.

Our basic premise is that we must stop pitting one group against another in the struggle to improve social policy. We believe that if an unmet need is effectively addressed, we all benefit, not just those who have that need at that particular time. Similarly, if that need is neglected and problems fester, we all pay, and we usually pay more by delaying. It is essential that we improve economic opportunities and strengthen social protections for our most vulnerable citizens. These themes are not antithetical but complementary, and they cut across all age groups.

Today's international economy challenges our capacity to produce, as more working-age Americans are affected by economic decisions that are made abroad. Changing family structures and growing areas of concentrated disadvantage challenge us to invest in all our nation's children. An aging population signals a need for us to rethink relationships between generations, and to confront the widening gap between the affluent and the impoverished elderly.

These new developments threaten to overwhelm a social welfare system that was created in the 1930s under very different social and economic circumstances. This system underwent steady, if incremental, expansion through the 1960s and 1970s, followed by retrenchment in the 1980s. Recently, social welfare policy has not kept up with a changing world. Many people now find themselves faced with personal crises they are wholly unprepared to resolve on their own, and for which government offers little help.

More than 30 million Americans live in poverty. About one-quarter of young Americans fail to finish high school. Children who are at greatest risk of failure in school are now the fastest growing segment of the school population and of the

1

future work force. The related phenomena of drug use and crime create a dangerous environment in urban America as well as a drain on our economy. The poor, and especially the elderly poor, are particularly vulnerable to these threats.

It is estimated that between 31 million and 37 million people lack any health insurance coverage and many others are underinsured. Most of these people are workers and their dependents. About half of our workers have jobs that do not provide private pensions, and such coverage of the work force has stopped growing. Meanwhile, unemployment insurance has become an increasingly threadbare component of the social safety net. Only about one-third of the unemployed receive such a benefit at any one point in time. As Americans live longer, they are more likely to need protection against the costs of long-term care for themselves and their family members; few are currently prepared for this eventuality.

Such problems signal a mounting social deficit that is as troubling as government budget deficits or the deteriorating physical infrastructure of roads and bridges. This report examines the shape and scope of that social deficit and offers a realistic, affordable program for addressing it in a comprehensive way. We should emphasize at the outset that we have found no quick or easy answers. The task of realigning the social welfare system with the needs of modern America will require efforts in the public and private sectors, a variety of methods, and many years. Most of all, it will require a realistic new consensus about our responsibilities to each other, now and in the future—a vision of where we are and where we want to go as a society.

There should be no illusions about the political difficulty of achieving such a consensus, especially in a time of budget deficits and general skepticism about public spending. Yet members of the project's executive panel agree that America has no choice but to try. As a result of years of neglecting our social infrastructure, the divisions in American society have increased in ways that threaten quality of life, peace of mind, and the economic future.

Lessons of Recent History

For much of America's history, social welfare needs were addressed exclusively through the family, voluntary organizations, and local governments. During the Depression, the nation discovered that this system, strong as it was, simply was not equal to the task of creating opportunity and protecting Americans' welfare without a more concerted, nationally based approach. The Federal government created new forms of social support to help reduce the insecurities that occur in every stage of life: Aid to Families with Dependent Children, Unemployment Insurance, and Social Security retirement benefits.

In subsequent years this base was steadily expanded to all social classes through a mixture of public and private efforts. The G.I. Bill made a college education available to millions. Public housing programs, Veterans Administration and Federal Housing Authority loans, tax rules, and a number of other housing subsidy programs helped millions afford home ownership. Encouraged by public policies, especially by changes in the tax code, the private sector extended the scope of social protection, offering employee fringe benefits like pension plans and health insurance. Washington stepped in again in the l960s with Medicare for the elderly and Medicaid for the poor.

In the l960s America also embarked on an even more ambitious experiment in offering opportunity to the disadvantaged. Congress passed such legislation as the Area Redevelopment Act and the Manpower Development and Training Act to focus on geographic "pockets of poverty" and workers left behind by structural changes in the economy. Encouraged by the civil rights movement, anti-poverty efforts concentrated on drawing disadvantaged persons into the labor market and breaking down barriers arising from racial discrimination or lack of education and skills. The diverse array of that era's programs included the Job Corps for poor teenagers, Head Start for preschoolers, civil rights legislation, and efforts to improve housing conditions and neighborhoods.

Not all the programs succeeded. Some were poorly conceived, promising more than reformers knew how to deliver. Others were well conceived but poorly implemented by our complex Federal system. Some efforts that were intended to expand opportunity wound up fostering dependency. For example, the l962 Manpower Development and Training Act originally placed a strong emphasis on skill training and private-sector job placement. By the 1970s the field was dominated by the Comprehensive Employment and Training Act (CETA) program, which was criticized for spending too much on income maintenance and too little on skill training and private-sector job placement.

In the l970s and 1980s the perception of failure in social welfare programs became widespread. Concern over the financial, social, and moral costs of dependency led some to claim that government had ceased to offer any answers to social problems and instead had itself become the problem, and that its attempts to help only interfered with private initiative and personal responsibility. Social protection, these critics asserted, ought to be left to private enterprise, charity, and voluntarism.

Yet political disputes over budgets and social programs in these years have made it clear that such attitudes do not reflect the priorities of the general public. Whatever faults they might perceive in social programs, Americans do not want to see them dismantled. Although many are concerned about the dependency of the poor, people at all levels have benefited from some government-supported social protections like Social Security, Medicare, and mortgage interest deductions. And it has remained clear that private charity and voluntarism, as important as they are, cannot fully meet the social needs of our citizens. Government participation is essential; we must learn from past experience how governments can respond more efficiently to the nation's social welfare needs.

Some lessons of that experience are obvious: Americans ought not to have to choose between the public and private sectors as avenues for dealing with problems of social welfare. Both are intimately linked; they should complement and support each other. Nor can we rely on economic growth alone to guarantee social welfare. A healthy economy, while essential, will not of itself generate the human investments and mutual caring that are necessary for a strong, just society. And while America has grown properly skeptical of programs that foster dependency, it has also learned that it is futile to ask people to take greater personal responsibility for their lives unless they have a real chance to escape from material conditions that foster insecurity and despair.

Years of experiment, success, and failure have also yielded a wealth of practical knowledge. We know, for example, what must be done to bring healthy babies into the world. We know that high-quality programs for preschool children pay dividends in later years. We know how to combine health, education, and family support services to help disadvantaged schoolchildren. We know that employment programs, though no panacea, can offer cost-effective improvements in the lives of many, including mothers on welfare.

Visions and Realities

An obvious conclusion arises from this accumulated knowledge. The best welfare policy offers individuals both economic opportunity and social protection, and it does so in a way that minimizes the waste of taxpayers' resources. Self-reliance ought to be encouraged, but it will be most effective within the context of a supportive social framework. Work is fundamental to an enlightened social welfare program, but people often need assistance in preparing for work, as well as some basic social support while they are working. At the same time, a government that offers help in the form of social programs must resist being exploited by people who will not try to help themselves. Nor should government waste money on programs that do not work.

We believe it is economically and socially prudent to design a policy that offers both opportunities and social protection for all American citizens. This is a way of recognizing that we are all interdependent. Today's poorly prepared preschoolers are tomorrow's marginal workers and nonworkers. Each of us will eventually depend on the skills and productivity of this emerging work force to maintain the country's economic competitiveness, to run an increasingly sophisticated national defense system, and to pay the Social Security bills in our old age. The poorly insured worker of today becomes tomorrow's indigent hospital patient, and society pays the tab by supporting the uncompensated health care that worker receives. Many families today are able to provide opportunities for their children precisely because their elderly parents are part of a system of protection that was created by our social insurance laws.

As taxpayers and as victims of a violent society we end up paying for the social wreckage that results from a lack of earlier investments in other people and their children. We cannot build enough prisons or buy enough home security systems to protect our private worlds from the social decay that spreads when true opportunity is denied to large numbers of people.

The panel believes that a union of individual opportunity and social protection makes sense in terms of how most Americans hope to lead their lives. Such a policy helps to define the kind of society in which we want to live.

Against this vision stands a sobering reality: in economic and social terms, America appears to be growing more divided rather than more united. In 1966, 45 percent of the public told pollsters they thought America was a place where "the rich get richer and the poor get poorer." By the late 1980s four out of five, 81 percent, agreed with that description of the country.

The public's impression seems all too accurate. The extent of inequality in individual earnings as well as in family incomes is greater today than it was twenty or thirty years ago. During the past decade we have made virtually no progress in reducing the poverty rate among the non-elderly population. As a nation, we are prosperous, but a substantial group of Americans live on the margins of that prosperity.

Several ongoing trends are likely to intensify such divisions. Growing competition in the international economic system is likely to force the United States to specialize increasingly in goods and services that require a highly skilled work force. The growth of knowledge-intensive jobs will leave a substantial group of Americans out in the cold unless we close the gap between the skills they possess and the requirements of a modern economy. Changing family structure may be similarly divisive. Prospects are bright for two-parent families in which one spouse devotes full time to a job that produces ample income and benefits like health insurance, while the other manages child care and other domestic duties and may also go to work to bring in more money. But this "typical" American family is shrinking in proportion to the population. More than half of the children born in America today will live in single-parent homes before age eighteen. Single parents find it much more difficult to manage work and child care and to link up with the opportunities and protections of the traditional labor market. For this and other reasons, nearly 25 percent of America's children under six now live in poverty. For minorities the percentage is 40 percent and both figures have been rising for more than ten years.

Persistent hard-core poverty among a small but growing proportion of our population has proven resistant to conventional remedies. Many of our inner-city areas contain isolated pockets of poverty, welfare dependency, joblessness, split families, crime, and drug use. All of these problems, of course, can be found throughout our society. But in some neighborhoods, their incidence is so high and their confluence so pronounced that young people growing up there have slim chances of succeeding in life.

The number of aged is rising in proportion to the total population. In twenty to twenty-five years, as the baby boomers retire, the aging of the population will be especially pronounced. Distribution of income and wealth among the aged is already more unequal than in the rest of the population. Such inequalities are more likely to grow than to diminish in the years ahead. Those who have been renters are much worse off than those who have owned homes and profited from the escalation of housing prices. The spread of employee benefits appears to have stopped well before reaching many low-wage earners.

These trends are especially worrisome because the current social welfare system appears oriented to picking up pieces rather than preventing the original breakage. Our policies typically do not help families with children until there is a crisis and the children are hurt. We spend large amounts to save the life of each low-birthweight baby, but skimp on the prenatal care that helps avoid future suffering. We stand aside as large numbers of children are damaged intellectually and socially in their first few years of life, and then rush in with remedial school programs and anticrime measures when the inevitable consequences of such neglect occur. We also ask the poor to go on welfare before health care is made accessible to them. We expect most jobless and very poorly paid workers to exhaust their unemployment benefits and their own resources before they can receive any help with retraining or other means of securing mobility in the labor market. We ask old people to "spend down"—a euphemism for impoverishing themselves—before assisting them with long-term care.

A more comprehensive strategy would be one that empowers people both in the workplace and in their varied family circumstances.

In the chapters that follow, we lay out specific recommendations that taken together would constitute a fundamental restructuring of social policy in America. Some of these recommendations would require new government spending. Others ask private enterprise to make a contribution. And some look to the voluntary sector for further help.

Solving the Funding Squeeze

Clearly, the scope for new government spending is limited in the years immediately ahead. As we shall show, however, it is possible to reallocate current revenues, so they are spent more wisely. We can also generate new revenue for much-needed social investments.

As we will discuss in Chapter 6, we found during our deliberations that one approach to financing the government's cost of meeting our agenda stood out as fair and sensible: The panel recommends that Social Security benefits exceeding an individual's lifetime contribution be subject to taxation. Such a step does not impose a "means test" on receiving Social Security. Rather, it permits all senior citizens to receive benefits, but recaptures a portion of benefits from higher-income people to help meet our nation's social welfare needs.

We do not view the full taxation of Social Security benefits as "hitting the elderly." It is a tax we will all pay one day when we become elderly. In other words, the elderly are not some group to be segmented and separated from the rest of us— they *are* us. Viewed from this perspective, the tax represents a way that we all can contribute to filling unmet social needs once we are in a position to pay it.

Furthermore, the panel feels strongly that the additional revenues generated by this taxation should be placed in a special fund, at least for a period of time, to be used to underwrite a portion of the cost of achieving a broad spectrum of social welfare goals. Eventually, we hope, we would not have to protect this fund but could treat it exactly like other revenue flowing into the Old Age and Survivors' Insurance (OASI) Trust Fund. During the next decade or two, however, as we reduce the "social deficit" described in this report, we must ensure that the new revenues match up directly with unmet needs across the age spectrum. In the short run at least, we see this as a sensible way to link the demand for taking action on the social deficit with the response to that demand.

The question that should be addressed is neither what is politically popular in the short run nor what "revenue-enhancing" gimmick can be found to pay the bills. The deeper issue is the need to create a fairer social system in which all will share both obligations and benefits.

Social Welfare and the Life Cycle

This report is organized according to the sequential phases of the life cycle: infancy and childhood, young adulthood, the working years, and old age. As the following vignettes suggest, a person's need for opportunity really begins before birth with prenatal care and extends through the retirement years. The same is true of a person's need for basic security.

A baby is born this year in an inner-city hospital, one of the majority who are destined to spend at least part of their childhood in a family headed by a woman. In theory the baby's future holds the equal opportunity open to all Americans at birth. In reality much will depend on the system of protections built around the child, by its family and by society at large. Will the baby be one of those already at a mental and physical disadvantage because of inadequate prenatal care or because their mothers were using crack? Will financial support from an absent father be forthcoming, and if not, will society help enforce the child's right to such support? Will decent day care and family services be available? Will the child grow up in a neighborhood where most adults have no jobs, crime is an everyday event, and most children are not functioning well by the time they enter kindergarten? Will the newborn baby live in a social milieu that protects its chance for a productive, rewarding life, or is it already condemned to dependency, poverty, and alienation?

A forty-five-year-old steelworker in Pennsylvania finds himself laid off because of foreign competition. Has the economy provided other jobs at decent wages? Is there unemployment insurance to help with the transition? If employers in the industry do not want an older worker, are retraining facilities available? Should illness strike, will the worker have good health benefits?

An eighty-year-old widow believes that she has lived long enough and worked hard enough to deserve respect and independence. She fears becoming an economic burden to her children. Has this elderly woman had a realistic opportunity to make financial provisions for her care should she no longer be able to function on her own? Must her protections be paid for by risking the economic well-being of her children and grandchildren?

It is a false dichotomy to picture opportunity as something only the young need and security the exclusive interest of the old. Senior citizens want opportunity also—not necessarily to work full time, but to maintain their independence, self-sufficiency, and dignity as long as possible. Similarly, a healthy breadwinner might seem able to do without the added measure of security—until a job disappears or an illness strikes.

Regrettably, the concept of opportunity has come to be associated with unassisted individualism and security with cradle-to-grave government protection. Neither of these approaches is what our country needs or what we call for. We believe in giving people a fair chance to succeed. This often requires giving them a boost to get on the ladder, as well as being there to catch them if they fall. The front-end boost and the protective net leave plenty of room for individual initiative. The individual is still expected to exert the energy to climb the ladder, and some will go higher than others. This is as it should be. But today some never even get to the first rung, and though we are all in danger of slipping, some never get a helping hand to get up again.

Each and every one of us has a stake in providing infants and young children, wherever they may live, the nutrition and emotional nurturing that allow them a decent start in life, both because it is right and because if we don't, they may burden us for decades with the costs of illness, dependency, and crime. All of us have a stake in helping adolescents and young adults make a successful transition from school to the increasingly demanding work force of the information age. All have an interest in retraining workers who are left behind by a changing economy so they will not be condemned to unproductive, dependent lives. And all can find personal reassurance in providing the elderly with freedom from the fear that an infirmity will devastate not only their health but also their family's financial and emotional underpinnings.

Such practical considerations argue strongly for the importance of dealing with the social deficit; the panel finds this effort to be not only right but also politically realistic. At the same time, there is a powerful moral reason to pursue the task. Social welfare policy is properly the concern of all Americans, not just because all may benefit from improving it but because improving it is the right thing to do. The moral integrity of our society depends in no small measure upon our ability to unite behind this belief.

With these considerations in mind, we will focus on infancy and childhood, the first phase of the life cycle.

Chapter Two

Infancy and Childhood:
A Time to Sow

There is no more important contradiction in social policy than this: From child-development research we now know that the first few years of life play a crucial role in shaping a person's lifelong mental, emotional, and physical abilities. And yet it is for this stage of life that we seem to make our social investments most grudgingly and tolerate the greatest deprivation. To illustrate:

- About one in five children lives in poverty.

- More than 12 million American children—the equivalent of a medium-sized country—are now poor.

- Some 3.3 million children are now living with their teenage mothers; the proportion of out-of-wedlock births to teenagers has soared during the past twenty years.

- Child abuse and neglect are growing; more than 2 million cases are reported each year, about 900,000 of which are verified.

Although scientific knowledge about early childhood years has mushroomed, it is during these years that Americans are most likely to live in poverty. Simply put, our knowledge is not being applied.

As parents, grandparents, aunts, uncles, and friends, most of us have peered through the glass of a hospital nursery at rows of infants wrapped in blankets—so vulnerable yet so full of promise. If we could somehow look through that window to view all the nation's children, the spectacle would be alarming. In a typical recent year we would see one-quarter of a million babies born undersized (i.e., weighing 5½ pounds or less), often afflicted by illness and handicaps. Some will die. In some inner-city hospitals more than one in ten babies are born drug-addicted. Forty-two percent of the white babies will live with a single mother by age eight, and most of these infants will experience a major spell of poverty during that time. Eighty-six percent of the black babies will live with a single mother by age eight, and most will be poor during most of that time. Many will grow up in an urban environment devoid of opportunity and full of danger. If current trends continue, more than of 40 percent of the Hispanic children will experience poverty before age eighteen. Although many will also live in households headed by women, a growing proportion of poor Hispanic children will live in two-parent families.

To summarize, we could look through the nation's nursery windows and separate the fortunate babies born to hope and safety from the unlucky babies—perhaps one in four—born threatened and suffering. The fortunate majority of infants can look forward to a long life span and a good standard of living. They will be well fed and decently housed, see a pediatrician regularly and receive all of the appropriate immunizations, attend good schools, never suffer child abuse or neglect, and be raised in relatively safe neighborhoods. The large number of unlucky babies will experience a childhood lacking in the essential requirements for good health, physical safety, and proper mental and social development. By the time they reach kindergarten, they will already be falling behind through no fault of their own. Anyone looking at the rows of infants in a hospital nursery and consciously advocating policies that deliberately produce such outcomes would rightly be branded a monster. Yet such is the effect of our current policies.

Investing in Infants

It is easy to generate sympathy, if not tax dollars, for infants born burdened and suffering through no fault of their own. A more hard-nosed case for increasing our investments in young children can be made by calculating the long-range benefits from the point of view of pure self-interest. We can pay a little now to try to prevent blighted childhoods or we can pay a lot later for the consequences. In other words, money for decent prenatal care, or more than three times as much to deal with low-birthweight infants; several thousand dollars for a good preschool program to open the mind of a ghetto three-year-old, or tens of thousands of dollars to cope with a hardened teenage criminal. At the same time, we in today's work force will eventually depend on the abilities and economic productivity of the infants being born today. In 1950 there were seventeen workers to support each older retired person; today there are 3.5 workers, and by the next century there will be only about two workers for each retiree. Finally, wasted childhoods will produce inadequate workers at a time when we can ill afford it, when growing competition in the world economy is increasingly forcing the United States to specialize in goods and services that require a highly skilled, adaptable work force.

Beyond the nation's economic competitiveness or the future security of retirees, crime, disorder, and other social pathologies are being set in motion now by what is happening to too many children. Today's infants are literally the nation's future. Whatever America can or will be is taking shape today in the nation's nurseries. The underlying challenge is clear enough, and so too are the social costs. The question of how to provide opportunity and social protection to children is complex, for the well-being of all young children must be a societal as well as a parental concern. Parents have primary responsibility for their children, but we all have an interest in healthy babies and in children's adequate nutrition and cognitive development. Moreover, the problems of infants are closely connected to issues we will deal with in subsequent chapters: teen pregnancy, gaps in health insurance coverage, joblessness, and underemployment of parents.

This chapter develops an agenda for reform in prenatal care, preventive health care and nutrition, early childhood development, and family support services. It is an agenda that emphasizes larger social investments in children at the earliest possible stages of life. These stages represent "windows of opportunity," and they do not stay open very long. Delay often means that by the time remedial help arrives, the window is already shut. The panel believes that it is simple common sense to make investments that are preventive and that capitalize on the earliest possible opportunities.

Extending Prenatal Care

Thanks to modern science, childbirth is not the mystery it once was. Bringing a healthy baby into the world is something we know how to do, but too often in America we fail to do it. We know the basic elements of a healthy start in life: prenatal care with regular screening to detect health risks, counseling to educate expectant mothers about appropriate health and nutritional habits during pregnancy, and continued good nutrition and health care for the newborn child. We know that pregnant women who obtain regular check-ups and periodic examinations by an obstetrician early in their pregnancies are more likely to have healthy babies than those who delay care until late in their pregnancy or do not obtain it at all.

Through measures such as these, the nation has made great strides in prenatal care and achieved dramatic reductions in infant mortality. The leading cause of infant death and handicaps, however, is still low birthweight resulting from a lack of adequate prenatal care and nutrition. Despite advances in medical technology, babies with low birthweights are almost forty times more likely to die in the first month than are normal-sized infants; for infants with very low birthweights (3.3 pounds or less), the risk of death is 200 times greater.

Two notes of caution should be sounded here. First, the value of prenatal care is clear for women in almost all age groups, but it is not so clear that even the best prenatal care can avert dangerous outcomes in the pregnancies of very young girls (i.e., less than fifteen years old). Their pregnancies will be risky under any circumstances, and the best policy is to devote our attention and resources to helping such young girls avoid pregnancy. Second, the wonders of modern medical technology may lead to a social policy dilemma: We are increasingly able to save the lives of even the smallest newborns (i.e., 1 1/2 pounds). We want people in all situations, including but not limited to the poor, to be able to avail themselves of lifesaving technologies, but we do not want these technologies to encourage the social behavior that triggers their use. The problem is complicated by the fact that underweight at-risk babies are found disproportionately among mothers who smoke, use drugs, and are very young; however, these babies can also be born to parents who have none of those characteristics.

Since the early 1950s the United States has achieved a reduction in its proportion of low-birthweight infants, but our percentage still remains one of the highest in the developed world. Moreover, there is a growing concentration of infant health problems among the poor, and the disparity between the life chances of white and nonwhite babies remains huge. Recent national data show that the infant mortality rate per 1,000 live births was 11.9 for white infants and 22.8 for black babies. Black births accounted for 16.5 percent of all live births, but for 30 percent of all low-birthweight babies, 34 percent of very low-birthweight births, and 28 percent of all infant deaths.

We have also learned that women with health insurance—either private or Medicaid—are more likely to seek prenatal care than women who lack coverage. At the same time, the women with the greatest risk of a low-birthweight delivery are those without health insurance and adequate prenatal care. During the 1980s the proportion of mothers who start prenatal care in the first trimester has stopped increasing and has possibly even declined.

It is reasonable to conclude that measures extending health insurance coverage to uninsured pregnant women can be expected to increase their use of primary and preventive obstetrical care. Furthermore, there is evidence that the additional outlays for insurance coverage would end up saving money in the long run. One careful study shows that an additional dollar spent on prenatal care saves an estimated $3.38 as a result of the reduced incidence of low-birthweight babies. The reduced suffering and the prevention of handicaps cannot be assessed.

At present, most families qualify for Medicaid by qualifying for the welfare rolls. State-by-state differences in eligibility standards for welfare assistance produce huge differences in access to health coverage. As a result, in many states poor families, even those living at less than half of the federal poverty standard, are effectively denied Medicaid because they are ineligible for welfare. More than 11 million American children are without private or public health insurance coverage, and half of all poor children are not covered by Medicaid. Yet, the babies in these families are at the greatest risk of being born weak and/or handicapped.

The Medicaid expansion provisions of the 1988 Medicare Catastrophic Illness legislation mark an important step in the right direction. This law grants Medicaid coverage to all pregnant women living in poverty and poor children below one year old. But a big problem remains: coverage for poor children above one year and poor adults who are screened out of Medicaid.

Studies also show that children receiving preventive care through the Medicaid Early and Periodic Screening, Diagnosis, and Treatment program (EPSDT) have fewer abnormalities and chronic health problems than nonparticipants. Preventive immunization and metabolic screening programs save as much as $14 for every dollar invested. Yet a significant and growing number of children in America are not receiving full immunization against preventable diseases. In 1980, 19.3 percent of two-year-olds had not been fully immunized against polio. By 1985 this figure had jumped to 23.3 percent, or nearly one child in five. Similarly, in 1985, 18.3 percent of two-year-olds had not received full immunization for measles; 22.7 percent for rubella; and 21.1 percent for mumps—all higher proportions than in 1980. Half of all black preschoolers are not fully immunized.

In a nation as wealthy as the United States, there is no good reason infants should be denied access to prenatal and well-baby care because their parents happen to live in one state rather than another, or have income just above rather than below an arbitrary welfare—or poverty—income line.

We propose a national commitment ensuring that all pregnant women have access to prenatal care and well-baby care. Health insurance coverage is part but not all of what is needed to fulfill this commitment. We also need to place greater emphasis on prevention and early detection of problems and on immunization even among those who have public and private insurance coverage.

Better Nutrition for Young Children

The logical next step is to improve the array of child and maternal services currently provided to low-income families. These services are offered through programs such as the Title V Maternal and Child Health Block Grant and, in particular, the Special Supplemental Food Program for Women, Infants, and Children (WIC).

WIC is a Federally financed program that provides screening, nutritional counseling, and food supplements for low-income pregnant women and for children up to age five who are diagnosed as nutritionally at risk. Under WIC, the U.S. Department of Agriculture allocates Federal funds to state health departments. These state agencies fund local health departments, hospitals, and health clinics to determine eligibility, offer education about nutrition, and prescribe proper foods for eligible recipients.

Several studies have found that this program can make a difference. Compared with similar groups of women who are not in the program, high-risk mothers in WIC tend to have a lower incidence of late fetal deaths and to deliver larger, healthier, less premature babies. The WIC newborns have larger head sizes, possibly implying better brain development. Babies and preschoolers in the program demonstrate superior cognitive development and less anemia than comparable infants and children who do not receive the assistance.

The payoff of WIC services seems clear, but our commitment to the program has been feeble. At present, states have the option of offering or not offering the WIC program to women with incomes of up to 185 percent of the poverty line. Because WIC is a discretionary program, states can and often do choose to serve only a limited number of those who are eligible and some states are reluctant to search vigorously for needy children who qualify for the program. Only about half of the eligible women and children are reached by the WIC program as it is currently constituted.

In recent years a few states (such as South Carolina and Massachusetts) have taken the initiative in trying to bolster the Federal WIC program with supplemental funding. As we will show later, a number of state and local models also seek to coordinate services to meet the multifaceted health and nutritional needs of young and vulnerable families. These efforts are laudable, but they must be bolstered by adequate investment at the national level so that services are available to all those who need them.

We recommend full funding for the WIC program as an entitlement for nutritionally at-risk women and children with incomes of up to 185 percent of the Federal poverty line. In addition to increased funding for WIC, greater attention should be paid to improving its basic management techniques. If ways can be found to economize on the use of resources, any given level of funding can be stretched to cover more people in need. Consider recent management innovations in the state of Texas. Instead of working with just one provider of food under WIC, the Texas state Board of Health opened the bidding and discovered that bringing a second bidder into the process saved $70 million over two years, as the second bidder offered the government a deeper discount. The state estimates that this will allow an additional 95,000 women, infants, and children to be served. Most states are now moving in the direction of competitive bidding.

WIC offers one more example of how children's good health and development require that different services be connected and made more accessible to parents and children together. For many low-income women, the main contact with government programs occurs when they enter a public hospital for labor and delivery. At this point they should have access to a system of referral to allied services, but by then their health and nutritional status is already seamlessly interwoven with that of their newborn. Pregnancy testing services should be linked to the food supplementation and nutrition system, which in turn must be connected to prenatal health care. And these strands of child-welfare policy must in turn be tied into what is happening to children with respect to day care and early child development. As we shall see, this is a challenging but not impossible set of connections to make.

More and Better Preschool Programs

Evidence accumulating during the last twenty years points strongly to the conclusion that high-quality development programs for disadvantaged preschoolers are among the soundest human investments. One does not have to be a certified child development expert to understand why. The early years of life are a critical period of development and learning, laying the groundwork for subsequent patterns of personality and intellect. Babies raised in a skilled, caring environment will generally differ from babies raised in a desensitizing, mind-numbing atmosphere. By the same token, three-, four-, and five-year-olds can be socially and intellectually deprived in a way that programs them for failure in the transition to school. Those early failures can then easily lead to a host of negative expectations and subsequent troubles. It should be emphasized that these circumstances are not the automatic result of living below a poverty income line or in a certain kind of family structure. Some single mothers with meager income are doing as much as one could ask of any parent, while some two-parent families with abundant resources are guilty of neglect.

The rising enrollment rates of three- and four-year-olds in preschool programs (from 21 percent of this age group in 1970 to 39 percent in 1985) testify to the widespread recognition of their value. The pattern of enrollment rates, however, indicates that early childhood education may be benefiting mainly the better-off children. Although more than half of higher-income families ($35,000 yearly income) enroll their three-year-olds in preschool programs, only 17 percent of three-year-olds from lower-income families ($10,000 or less) are in preschools. Yet it is precisely among poorer infants and children that the need for preschool experience is greatest, and it is among them that the evidence is strongest for the major positive impact of good early childhood development programs.

The types of targeted social investments we need to make will vary somewhat across the age span of young children. In general, we should move our resources to where the children are actually spending their days. In recent years, four- and five-year-olds are often connected to the public school system, which increasingly reaches out for these preschool children with part-day programs. On the other hand, one- and two-year-olds are usually not going to come in contact with the public schools or the Head Start program. Yet the more we learn, the more critical it appears that there be skilled development-enhancing care during these earliest years; by eighteen months some infants are already in need of remedial help. Because the child is often in a home during these years, the problem could be addressed with an effective program of home visits along with parent and caregiver education.

What good preschool child development programs do is help tilt the odds for poorer children away from failure and toward success. Studies show that quality programs help improve these children's social preparation and intellectual performance when school begins. There is less need for special education programs or repeating grades. The likelihood of completing high school, gaining college or vocational training, and holding a job is significantly increased. The few existing in-depth, long-term studies show that good-quality preschool development programs can improve poor children's achievement throughout the school years, reduce their delinquency and arrest rates, and also reduce the rates of teenage pregnancy and dependence on welfare.

A careful analysis of one such program, the Perry Preschool Project, studied both costs and benefits over the years. In the early 1960s black three- and four-year-olds from poor families in a single Michigan school district were randomly divided into two groups. One group participated for one to two years in a program of high-quality early childhood education; the other did not. After that, nothing else was done for either group as they grew up in a typically impoverished setting. Although the sample size in this experiment was small, the results suggest that the benefits to the participants and to the taxpayers were positive by the time the children were nineteen. For an initial investment of $5,000 per participant per program year, there were the following savings (in constant dollars) when compared with non-participants:

- $3,000 savings per child in reducing the costs associated with delinquency and crime

- $5,000 savings in special education or remedial programs later in school

- $16,000 savings in public assistance

- $5,000 more in taxes collected because of better employment and earnings

By the time the children who participated in the original 1961 Perry Preschool Project were in their middle to late twenties, the benefits of that small, early investment had continued to compound.

Other studies from the Head Start program and the New York longitudinal project have tended to confirm these results. The Perry project dealt with a small city environment (Ypsilanti, Mich.). The New York project, conducted by the Institute for Developmental Studies, operated with inner-city youths from New York City. Beginning in the mid-1960s, a program of educational enrichment was offered for up to five years to a sample of children starting at four years of age. The long-term payoff in jobs and education at ages nineteen to twenty-one becomes clear in relation to control groups that did not participate in the program. The results are remarkably comparable to the findings from Michigan (see Figure 2.1).

It is important to recognize that quality is as important as quantity in early childhood education programs. There is no evidence that developmental gains result simply from sending a young child out to be with another adult and a group of children in a classroom or a child-care center. Effective investment in disadvantaged preschoolers depends on both continuous parent involvement and well-designed, well-run programs of early childhood education. The essential components are staff with specific training in early childhood development and education and a knowledge of preschoolers' needs; adequate resources to provide the necessary services; group sizes that are appropriate to a classroom or a child-care center; and, for Hispanic children with limited proficiency in English, staff trained to help them as well as special bilingual or English-as-a-Second-Language materials. Trying to impose formal academic standards on young children through a traditional school curriculum is not what is needed. Neither is it good enough simply to dump disadvantaged preschoolers into day-care centers where there is no proven educational plan behind the day's activities. The multifaceted kinds of day care and the more promising programs of early childhood development must be combined into an integrated system.

The nation's primary national program for disadvantaged preschoolers is Head Start, which was created in 1965. Through a variety of local organizations, Head Start offers a wide mix of programs. There are literally stacks of evaluation studies demonstrating that high-quality Head Start programs do change young people's lives, and we know what is needed to strengthen less effective programs: well-trained teachers, validated childhood development curricula, hands-on supervision, and parental involvement.

Although funding for the Head Start program was not cut in the early 1980s, there still have not been nearly enough funds to train and compensate personnel, much less to meet the needs of disadvantaged three- and four-year-olds, or to provide even a small part of the services needed by low-income parents and infants below the age of three. Today, for example, about 2.5 million poor children—28 percent of all those of preschool-age—are eligible for Head Start, but because of funding limits, only one in five of these children is currently enrolled in the program. Thus, while an increasing majority of upper-income families are sending

Figure 2.1 Job and Educational Status of 19- to 21-Year-Olds With and Without Preschool Development Program Participation

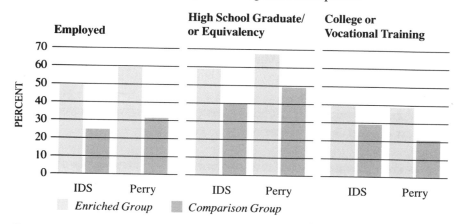

Source: Martin Deutsch, Theresa J. Jordan, and Cynthia P. Deutsch, *Long-Term Effects of Early Intervention,* Institute for Developmental Studies, 1985.

their children to the best early childhood education programs that money can buy, the vast majority of already disadvantaged children are losing ground before they have even reached the school system.

During the 1980s somewhat less than half the states have initiated or expanded their own early childhood education programs. Some of these funds go to Head Start agencies, but there is an increasing tendency to use the public school systems as well. By 1987 only about 100,000 children were served by these state-sponsored early childhood education programs; more than half were in the two states of California and Texas. As a small fraction of its enrollees, Head Start has also begun to include preschoolers who are educationally disadvantaged regardless of income status. In some localities greater efforts are being made to provide training in early child development to mothers who care for children at home. High-quality early childhood education programs can occur in a variety of settings under many different auspices. Despite this diversity, it is nonetheless important to scale up and institutionalize successful Head Start models in order to help larger numbers of disadvantaged children.

One way to do this is to institutionalize Head Start in the public schools. The states should be encouraged to think of Head Start as an early childhood education program, rather than as an antipoverty program that is outside their public education jurisdiction. It is important to link an expansion of Head Start with the process of reaching out to preschool children that is now occurring in the public schools.

Not everything can be done at once. That fact, however, must not be allowed to distract from the fundamental, long-term goal: to make quality, early childhood development services available to all preschool children who are at risk of failure in school. Today's children deserve, and the nation needs, direct action now toward that goal.

We recommend a major expansion of the Head Start program. Our ultimate goal is to make Head Start available to all families who need and want to use it. The specific long-range objectives are:

- **to provide enough slots for the 80 percent of poor three- and four-year-olds who are now denied this service;**

- **to make at least one-half of these slots full-day programs for children with working parents;**

- **to expand family-support, referral, and home-visiting services to very low-income parents, especially teen mothers, with children below age three;**

- **to increase funding for improved staff compensation and staff training in early childhood development**

- **to address the needs of children whose knowledge of English is limited.**

It is unrealistic to think of achieving these goals in one year's time. They represent targets toward which we hope to move incrementally. The section on costs at the end of this chapter lays out a realistic near-term goal.

Improving Day Care

Changing economic and household arrangements are creating a new kind of vulnerability for many young families today. Not long ago the daytime care and nurturing of young children was centered in the household. Today more women with young children are entering the paid labor force either of necessity or by choice. About one-third of the women with preschool children work full time, and when those working part time are included, the proportion is more than half.

Although the number of licensed day-care centers has grown rapidly during the past decade, the growth in supply has not fully met the needs of either two-earner families or single-parent households. Nor has enough attention been paid to the quality of day care. In addition, the average cost of child care, an estimated $3,000 per year (full time), is beyond the means of many lower-income families, even with existing Federal assistance programs and the child-care tax credit.

America has not had as much experience with day care as with child health and nutrition, which makes it more difficult to offer social policy recommendations. Yet there is an urgent need for comprehensive policy in this area: Our society places a high value on the proper care and nurturing of children; good day-care services play an important role in helping parents earn the income that is necessary to a stable household; and there is a widespread need for day care among families at all income levels.

The goals of such a policy should be to increase the availability of quality day care, to help families with financial need defray the cost, and to assure the safety and well-being of children without unnecessarily impeding the provision of adequate care. Meeting these goals will require the participation of federal, state, and local governments, as well as private-sector employers, voluntary associations, and families.

Some families currently receive assistance with day care from their employers, but day care remains the employee benefit that is least frequently offered. The number of employers providing on-site information-referral services has grown more than 400 percent since 1983; however, only an estimated 3,000 of 6 million private employers provide some kind of day care.

A small number of families are receiving day-care services funded by Title XX Social Services Block Grants. The income tax system offers broader Federal assistance. It allows tax credits for day-care expenses and does not tax employer benefits. These tax benefits tend to favor middle- and upper-income families, however, and do little for working families near the poverty line with little income tax liability. Such families are often on the borderline that separates work from welfare, so that extending them some tax relief could provide the difference that would make them self-sufficient.

We recommend that the Federal government provide child-care subsidies for lower-income families through such steps as making the existing tax credit refundable. We also recognize that providing adequate day care is not just a matter of financing, but also concerns assurances of safety and an adequate supply of services. State and local governments can play an important role here by establishing certification and monitoring mechanisms that are more rigorous in enforcing safety standards. At the same time, however, local authorities should review existing zoning requirements to eliminate unnecessary barriers that now prevent day care from taking place in safe settings like homes or churches. Unrealistic specifications about the number of toilets in a home, for example, might block a mother from offering day care to four children in a safe home setting, while zoning rules may permit day care in a dangerously run-down commercial neighborhood.

A commitment to quality care must also be reflected in the compensation of day-care workers. Currently, they are in the lowest 10 percent of all wage earners, and many have no health benefits. Steps to improve their training, wages, and benefits should be linked to community-wide efforts to set and uphold standards for day-care centers.

Stronger Child Welfare Services

Improved prenatal, nutrition, preschool, and day-care services promise a brighter future for American children in years to come, but no child-welfare policy can be considered complete unless it addresses the young victims who are now suffering from neglect, abuse, abandonment, and homelessness. Their circumstances reflect a general pattern of failed family-support services. A distressingly large and growing number of children spend their early years in brutalizing and dangerous circumstances. The two million cases of child abuse now reported per year are approximately four times the 516,000 cases reported in 1977. At least another quarter of a million are in state-sponsored substitute care—foster homes, group homes, or institutions. By failing to stem the abuse and neglect from which these children are suffering, we sow the seeds of future violence and dependency.

Many of these problems overlap with the growing number of homeless people in America. Children have been joining the ranks of the homeless in increasing numbers. Here surely are the most vulnerable of all America's children. Most homeless children are of preschool age. Many are suffering abuse and neglect at the hands of parents who themselves were victims of violence and neglect as children. And although studies of homeless children often focus on small samples in only a few places, there is growing evidence that there are children whose medical, nutritional, educational, and emotional needs are woefully unmet. The problem of homelessness is the most poignant and troubling part of a much larger problem that includes the difficulty many families, especially young families, have in affording decent housing today.* This problem cannot be adequately addressed without considering ways to increase the supply of low-income housing, reform the income maintenance system, and improve access to health and social services.

Still, the present system of child-welfare services deserves attention. It is a maze of overlapping program jurisdictions and fragmented services, geared to addressing crises after they occur rather than averting them. Existing family services are designed to come into play mainly after children have experienced some severe and often traumatizing problem—abuse, illness, abandonment, poverty, retardation, and so on. Athough this emergency approach is important for children in immediate danger, it is inadequate for dealing with the overall stresses of con-

---

*A full-scale review of the housing problem is beyond the scope of this report. Recent findings and recommendations contained in the report *A Decent Place to Live: The Report of the National Housing Task Force* (commissioned by Senators Alan Cranston and Alfonse D'Amato and chaired by James Rouse) offer a realistic blend of public policy reforms and private-sector initiatives. The task force report acknowledges that the problem of affordable housing is not experienced exclusively by the poor, and that we need a mixture of policy reforms to help a broad range of Americans—assistance to the poor in conjunction with measures aimed at helping lower-to-middle-income young families gain a foothold in the housing market.

Particularly significant is the recognition of diverse local housing initiatives that have originated across the nation in recent years. Central to these efforts are new community development corporations and other "self-help" groups that could become part of a more flexible, decentralized delivery system for housing and community development. This new system amounts to a grass-roots infrastructure that can be nurtured with renewed Federal assistance. Such a system offers clear advantages over the mammoth, prescriptive Federal housing programs of the past.

temporary family life. We must find new ways of detecting the early warning signs of families and children in trouble. We must give parents information about how to cope with problems at home and where to go in the community to find services they need. Any realistic social welfare policy for the future should not be geared exclusively to "problem children" and "problem families," but to all families that, left stranded without support, are candidates for trouble.

Besides a child-abuse program, homeless services, or foster care, such support must necessarily involve related systems of medical care, education, nutrition, mental health, and early childhood development. Since the enthusiastic reforms of the 1960s, we have learned painfully that such coordination of services does not easily occur with a top-down organizational structure. It occurs more effectively at the community level—a local neighborhood or church group, a Head Start office, a hospital, a social service agency. In various parts of the country today, promising experiments seek the integration of educational, medical, housing, and child-protection services.

The Lafayette Courts Family Development Center, located in one of Baltimore's largest public housing high-rise developments, serves a population of 805 family units containing more than 500 children below age six. Eighty-five percent of the families are on welfare and 44 percent of the adults did not complete high school. The program aims to provide the entire family unit with a structured and comprehensive plan of services and support. Case managers work with each family to arrange an appropriate mix of services. They include:

- developmental child-care services, with on-site Head Start programs for children up to age three; full-day child care, and an after-school center with enrichment programs;

- on-site health services, with a well-child and adolescent clinic, prenatal care, immunization, and scheduled screening and referral for adults;

- adult education classes, including general equivalency degree courses on site and advanced courses at Morgan State College;

- employment services, with job-readiness workshops, employment counseling, testing and referral for occupational training, and a school-year summer jobs program for teenagers;

- family-support counseling, with workshops on parenting and family stress.

This coordination requires that someone pull together a host of different funding streams and programs. In the case of the Lafayette Family Center, officials in the city public housing authority also have been able to play the role of landlord, offering services that are a mixture of new and redirected resources. Private philanthropy has renovated the building to permit on-site services. Other capital costs and some operating expenses come from Community Development Block Grants. Employment and training services are funded out of the Federal Job Training Partnership Act. Day-care slots are jointly budgeted from state Investment in Job Opportunities funds and the Purchase of Care program in the Department of Social Services. The Health and Recreation Departments provide in-kind services and help with contracting out.

Another promising experiment is the widely publicized Beethoven Project in Chicago. Begun with support from both the U.S. Department of Health and Human Services and the Harris Trust, this project targets about 150 infants born in six high-rise buildings of the nation's largest public housing complex, children who will eventually attend the neighborhood's Beethoven Elementary School. The preparation of this future kindergarten class of 1993 begins before birth with prenatal care for the mothers. Health screening and continued health services follow after birth, together with day care, nutritional aid, and counseling for parents in child development. At age three the children will be enrolled in Head Start.

Learning from State Experience

By no means should family-support centers be regarded as limited to public housing or welfare clients in urban settings. In the past four years six states have initiated programs to extend their preventive resources to a wide variety of families. In Missouri, the Parents as Teachers program reaches 53,000 families; participation is open to any parent with a child under three. Monthly home visits and group discussion meetings among parents offer guidance on good child-development practices, while identifying and referring children who show signs of developmental problems. In Kentucky, a state where nearly half of the adults lack a high school degree, the Parent and Child Education Project offers parents and preschool children in twelve rural districts an opportunity to develop together. The program includes parent education and tutoring three days a week for a high school equivalency diploma.

Probably the most extensive state effort is Maryland's three-year-old system of Family Support Centers. This statewide network of eleven local centers is funded and guided by a public-private partnership composed of the state's Department of Human Resources, private foundations, and local communities. An umbrella non-profit corporation, Friends of the Family, coordinates the effort. Centers are community-based, with drop-in facilities aimed especially at serving all young families with children under age three. The centers offer parenting education, ongoing child-development assessment, help with education and job skill training for parents who lack schooling, access to health care (prenatal, reproductive, well-baby, etc.), developmentally appropriate child care, and assistance in arranging outside day care. The emphasis is on increasing parents' capacities to care for their children so as to prevent problems from reaching the crisis stage.

These programs should not be oversold. There are few research results on them and no guarantee that every one will register clear success in changing children's lives. The best programs, such as Maryland's, contain a central intermediary body that controls the standards of service and staffing and issues ongoing evaluations. These experiments could be testing grounds for the rest of the nation's social welfare practices, while national and state government policies could facilitate such experimentation and learning. The basic outline seems clear enough: Our systems of health care, nutrition services, day care, and child development should be connected and delivered to those children and parents who need them the most.

We recommend that state and local governments make a major effort to test and implement new approaches to family-support services that feature effective early intervention, parent education, and careful coordination of diverse public programs. We need a better link between government services at the state and local levels and private voluntary organizations.

The Federal government also has an important role to play in child welfare, and we recommend that steps be taken to:

- **provide adequate funding of programs like Social Services Block Grants, AFDC-Foster Care, those in the Child Abuse Prevention and Treatment Act, and those in the child-welfare services provisions of the Social Security Act;**

- **increase support for research on child-welfare problems at the National Institute of Child Health and Human Development;**

- **offer financial and informational support to state governments and local entities to help them improve their services to children in need and prevent the need for such services in the first place.**

The Cost of Our Proposals

The estimated cost to the Federal government of the recommendations in this chapter is $6.2 billion. We have indicated that two Federal programs geared to infants and children—WIC and Head Start—should be extended to a much broader group of children in need of help. In fiscal year 1988 Federal outlays for the WIC program totaled about $1.8 billion, and the program served 3.4 million people. The maximum potential number of people who could qualify for the program has been estimated at 6.5 million to 7.5 million, or about twice the number served today. If WIC were made an entitlement program, and all of the people eligible on income grounds actually qualified and participated, its cost would increase by $1.5 billion to $2 billion a year.

WIC. Households are eligible for WIC if they qualify as nutritionally at risk and have incomes up to 185 percent of the Federal poverty line. It is probable that in practice the population that participated would be limited by the nutritional-risk requirement and the likelihood that some who are eligible would not participate. Thus, the actual additional cost of making WIC an entitlement program would likely be less than the amounts noted above. To be on the safe side, however, we will assume that current costs double, and allocate an additional $1.7 billion for WIC outlays (see Figure 2.2).

Head Start. The Head Start program serves about one in five children aged three to five years old who are living in poverty, and only about one-fifth of those served are in full-day programs. Additional funding for the Head Start program could be used to cover more children, increase the proportion of children receiving full-day services, and extend coverage to children under three years old.

A report by the Congressional Budget Office suggested that the long-range impact of Head Start on such goals as increasing basic skills, avoiding crime, and finding employment is unclear as a result of the difficulty of finding adequate control groups. But the report pointed out that Head Start potentially could serve a number of more immediate purposes, including providing high-quality child care to children of working parents; increasing access to health screening, immunization, and a variety of social services; providing helpful cognitive stimulation to the children; offering employment and training to low-income adults; and making it possible for two parents to work.

Expanding Head Start will be more expensive than expanding WIC. The annual cost per child served under Head Start has been estimated at $2,400, compared with a little less than $500 for WIC. Serving as many needy children as possible through Head Start involves scaling up the program to serve the 80 percent not being served now, as well as having more children in full-day programs.

It is difficult to put a precise price tag on this effort at scaling up. Clearly, some parents of eligible children may choose not to enroll them in Head Start programs. Other eligible children may already participate in state and local programs or may have started kindergarten. A realistic goal for the early 1990s is to serve half of the eligible population that is not being served now. We estimate that it will cost $2 billion to meet that goal (see Figure 2.2).

Figure 2.2 Summary of Government Outlay Increases for Proposals to Help Children

Program	Outlay Increase	New Recipients
WIC	$1.7 billion	3.4 million*
Head Start	2.0 billion	0.9 million
Medicaid	1.0 billion	2.0 million
Chapter 1	1.5 billion	1.0 + million**
Total	**$6.2 billion**	7.3 million

*Assumes that most of the people eligible on income grounds will qualify and participate

**Rough estimate; the benefits of additional outlays are more students and longer periods of help per student

Health. Ultimately, all children and pregnant women in families below the poverty line ought to be covered by either Medicaid or a private health insurance policy. We are reluctant to advocate expanding Medicaid to the entire poverty population, which includes many families headed by a worker whom we hope to see covered under private health insurance (see Chapter Four).

The Medicare catastrophic illness legislation passed by Congress in 1988 includes provisions that make more low-income pregnant women and children under one year of age eligible for Medicaid. This is a useful first step, but we need to go much further. There are approximately 12 million to 13 million people living below the poverty line without health insurance. About 4 million of these are children under eighteen years of age. An estimated one-half of these children would qualify for the type of mandatory private coverage that we advocate below. The cost of providing Medicaid coverage to the remaining group of low-income uninsured children is approximately $1 billion (see Figure 2.2). It is important to note that this new coverage is "Medicaid only." It is not an extension of Aid to Families with Dependent Children (AFDC). We do believe that AFDC eligibility requirements should be updated. But we do not believe that an extension of Medicaid should be tied to AFDC.

Ideally, both Medicaid and employer-sponsored group health insurance ought to be broadened to assure health coverage for all Americans. It is important to put some restrictions on cash welfare assistance in order to maintain the incentive to work, though this goal can be met with higher cash assistance benefits than now exist in some states. But health coverage for the poor ought not to be held hostage to these necessary restrictions on cash assistance.

Chapter 1. Chapter 1 of the Education Consolidation and Improvement Act of 1981 funds compensatory education programs for low-income and educationally deprived students. Evaluations of the Chapter 1 program have shown positive short-term effects on student performance, and some evidence suggests a favorable longer-term impact.

The real level of outlays per poor child for this program has fallen in recent years, as slight absolute increases in funding have not kept pace with the combination of inflation and the higher number of children living in poverty. The proportion of poor children served by Chapter 1 fell from 75 percent in 1980 to 54 percent in 1985. Outlay increases of $1.5 billion per year would make up most of the erosion in real benefits per poor child associated with inflation, and enable many school districts either to extend services to some newly poor children or maintain services for a longer part of some children's schooling (see Figure 2.2). That might help avoid the erosion of shorter-term gains that has been found in some evaluations.

Conclusion

Neither we nor any other group have solutions for all the profound problems of social welfare that shape the earliest stages of life in America. The amount of new government spending that we have recommended to help children in need—$6.2 billion—would go a long way toward meeting the needs of disadvantaged children. It is worth noting, however, that the recommended budget would not extend help to each and every child in need—a reflection of current budget realities and the value of learning as we go. We believe this investment in better opportunities for American children will produce great future benefits for our whole society.

Chapter Three

Young Adulthood:
Preparing for a World of Work

Too many young Americans are failing to make an adequate transition from school to work. They drift aimlessly through their young adulthood—often with disastrous consequences. There has been a growing inequality between the prospects of those who attend college and those who do not. The latter are finding it increasingly difficult to obtain a decent job, start a career, and support a family.

Approximately one in four American teenagers leaves high school before receiving a diploma, and dropout rates are higher for minorities. An estimated 40 percent of Hispanic students leave before finishing high school, and among blacks in some urban areas the dropout rate is climbing toward 50 percent. Some individuals manage to obtain a high school equivalency degree later; however, there has been no progress in reducing the overall dropout rate during the last decade. High school dropouts are $2\frac{1}{2}$ times more likely than graduates to be without a job, $3\frac{1}{2}$ times more likely to be arrested for a crime, and $7\frac{1}{2}$ times more likely to be dependent on public assistance.

Young males with less than a college education have had trouble in the labor market during the past fifteen years. The real value of their earnings has fallen sharply, their job prospects have become more marginal, and their ability to support a family above poverty levels has diminished. The proportion of eighteen- to twenty-four-year-olds counted "inactive"—i.e., not employed, not enrolled in school, and not in the military—has almost doubled during the past twenty years to approximately 12 percent for white males, and more than doubled to almost 30 percent for nonwhite males.

For girls, pregnancy is the most important reason for leaving school. By age twenty, approximately 20 percent of white teenagers and 45 percent of black teenagers have been pregnant—one of the highest rates of pregnancy for teenagers in the developed world. Because of the greater prevalence of abortions and contraception, fewer teenage girls are having babies today than thirty years ago, but more and more teenage mothers are unmarried and remaining so. The proportion of babies born out of wedlock to white girls between the ages of fifteen and nineteen rose from 6 percent in 1955 to 49 percent in 1986; for black girls, the proportion increased from 41 percent to 90 percent; for Hispanics the current figure is 45 percent. Teenage mothers are half as likely to graduate from high school as are other girls. The children of "child-mothers" generally have lower achievement scores, are more likely to repeat school grades, and are more frequently on welfare than other children.

Though today's labor market is tightening, the economic situation facing young adults *as a group* is improving because a smaller cohort of young people is entering the market. But because of the increasing skill requirements of jobs in all sectors of the economy, the cost of being poorly prepared for work is much higher than it was a decade or two ago. The problem today is not so much a lack of jobs, but rather a growing mismatch between the skill requirements of jobs and the skills that many young people bring to the labor market.

Experience has shown that skill training is not all that is required to reach many young people who are completely disconnected from our institutions of education and work. Reaching these youths requires finding ways to motivate them to have goals in life and to aspire to success. It also involves helping some of them obtain treatment and overcome problems related to alcohol and drug addiction. We should not underestimate the difficulty of these challenges.

The trends outlined above represent an immense challenge to the American systems of education, training, and social welfare—systems that are grounded in the concepts of work and personal effort. Through gainful employment, Americans expect and are expected by society to be able to make their way in the world and to build the first line of defense against the inevitable hazards of life. To enter adulthood unprepared for the world of work is to see access to opportunities and job-related protections slipping away.

Compound Problems, Intertwined Answers

The trends are ominous. A growing undereducated subgroup of teenagers will soon become a growing and underprepared work force.

Demographic trends indicate that the youth cohort—sixteen- to twenty-four-year-olds—is diminishing in size. By 1995 there will be fewer Americans in this age group than there were in 1979. At the same time, the pace of technological change and growing international economic competition demand that this smaller work force also be more educated, skilled, and productive.

The evidence indicates that this challenge will confront a work force containing a higher proportion of young adults from disadvantaged backgrounds. Given differences in fertility rates and immigration patterns, it is likely that by the year 2000, the proportion of sixteen- to twenty-four-year-olds who are in racial or ethnic minority groups will increase from one in six to almost one in three. Minority and economically disadvantaged youths today are much more likely to drop out of high school. If they do stay to obtain their diplomas, the education they have received generally compares poorly with that available in suburban schools and affluent neighborhoods. Minority and poor youth are concentrated in the bottom fifth of the score distribution on virtually every major standardized test used in this country. At the same time, college enrollment rates for blacks and Hispanics declined from the 1970s to the 1980s.

There was a time when many poorly educated teenagers could eventually make the transition from school to work through blue-collar manufacturing jobs and craft apprenticeships. Since the early 1970s structural economic changes have severely reduced this segment of the youth labor market. Today those whose formal schooling stops with high school are entering the service and retail trade sector of the economy at almost the same rates at which college-educated youths entered this sector in 1960. But the jobs the high school graduates find are now more often in the low-paid, unstable, dead-end segments of the service economy.

The problem is especially severe among young black males, but by no means is it confined to one race. In 1974 nearly half of the employed black men aged twenty to twenty-four were in what could be considered career manufacturing jobs (blue-collar craft, operative, foreman work); the real median income of black males in that age group had risen 68 percent since 1959. By 1984 only about one-quarter of black males of that age were in such jobs, and the real income for this age group had fallen 44 percent since 1973. For white males of the same age, real median income had risen 28 percent from 1959 to 1973 and fallen by 32 percent between 1973 and 1984.

There are really two stories here (see Figure 3.1). One has to do with the general sluggishness of U.S. economic performance from the early 1970s to the mid-1980s, and the way this adversely affected the incomes of all young people. From the 1950s to the early 1970s, each successive cohort of young workers could look forward to doing better than its predecessors. Because of the slowdown in U.S. economic growth after 1973, this is no longer true.

The second story concerns the growing split among young adults engaged in the transition from school to work. Since 1973 those with a college education have been better able to hold their own and in their later twenties even bounce back from earlier economic troubles. However, young people with only a high school diploma or less have seen their income positions continue to erode. By 1986—during the

Figure 3.1 Real Median Annual Earnings for Males in Their Twenties, by Schooling and Selected Years

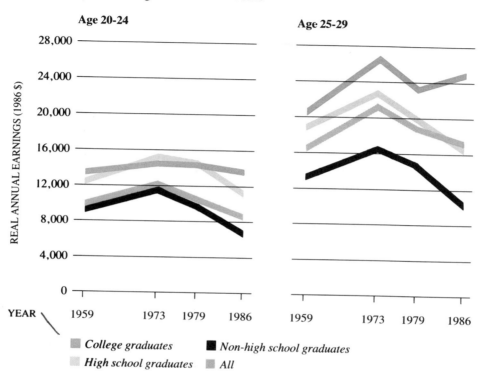

Source: Andrew Sum, Neal Fogg, and Robert Taggart, *Withered Dreams: The Decline in the Economic Fortunes of Young, Non-College Educated Male Adults and Their Families* (prepared for the William T. Grant Foundation Commission on Family, Work, and Citizenship, April 1988), Table 7, p.A-5.

fourth year of an economic recovery—young males with only a high school degree actually were earning 7 percent to 10 percent less than their counterparts had earned in 1959. Those without the degree were earning 20 percent to 25 percent less than their 1959 counterparts. Between 1959 and 1979, male college graduates between the ages of 25 and 29 earned 15 percent to 18 percent more than high school graduates of the same age. By 1986, the gap had grown to 51 percent.

Behind the bare statistics lies a complex pattern of social disorder. Changes in the U.S. economy are dealing a severe blow to the earnings capacity of many young men, particularly those with limited education and skills. This is one important factor in the formation of young families, as it dims the marriage prospects for young mothers and strains those two-parent families in which the breadwinners lack basic skills. The disadvantaged children of unwed mothers and poor two-parent families have become a growing proportion of the nation's future work force.

Between 1974 and 1985, the poverty rate for children in families headed by persons aged twenty to twenty-four rose from approximately 25 percent to almost 50 percent. A growing proportion of those families are headed by mothers who have never been married. Their limited schooling and their predicament as sole earners in the modern labor market mean that nearly 90 percent of their children are growing up in poverty. The web of misfortune does not touch only families headed by women. Among married couples headed by a man with only a high school education, a child poverty rate that was 6.8 percent in 1973 had tripled to 21.6 percent by 1986. In the years ahead, all of these disadvantaged children will be the ones with the most meager prospects for educational attainment and real economic independence.

It is important to emphasize that growing numbers of young Americans are trapped by a complex of interconnected problems: leaving school early, teen parenthood, welfare dependency, joblessness, delinquency, and an unstable family life. Too often in the past, attention and resources have shifted from one thread to another, with efforts directed at dealing with the concern of the moment—delinquency, illegitimacy, poverty, welfare dependency, unemployment, inadequate schooling. These efforts have led to a growing recognition that those in greatest need are suffering from not just one problem but many, and that greater effort, more resources, and more time will be needed to help them.

We view this complex problem as the Achilles heel of our society. Many approaches to dealing with disadvantaged youth have proved promising—one-on-one mentoring, after-school remedial help, summer jobs, and others. But when all is said and done, we must soberly admit that we simply do not have any magic answer for reaching young people. We know that training helps, but it is not a panacea. We know that values and motivation are important, but these elements cannot be imposed from the outside—they must grow from within a community.

In short, we can and should do all we can to prepare our youth, to lead them to the starting line. But we cannot run the race for them. The motivation to do this must come from within. Unhappily, there is no quick solution for interwoven problems that have been generations in the making. By urging recognition of this fact we are not counseling despair but realism. The first step is to transcend the intellectual stereotypes and divisions of the past.

Many local communities, neighborhood and church groups, private businesses, and grass-roots leaders have become more realistic in their approach to pressing social problems. Should programs for school dropouts or teen pregnancy be preventive or rehabilitative? Any sensible program must be both. Should initiatives be public or private? Again the answer from the front lines is that public institutions like schools must work more closely than ever before with private business leaders and volunteer groups. Should we have national or local programs? Once again, realism demands both. Without an adequate and sustained flow of national resources, local initiatives in poor communities too often die for lack of funds; without the commitment of local leaders, the programs remain empty bureaucratic shells.

This chapter offers no blueprint for all communities to follow. However, the essential concept is clear enough: Expanding the future life options of young men and women who are troubled by multiple problems requires more than one-dimensional treatments of particular symptoms. Effective programs must offer help that embraces basic skills, training (including English as a Second Language for Hispanics and others), employment, pregnancy prevention, and realistic planning for the future. No program can prevent all individual misfortunes, but policies can and should try to prevent problems from compounding to the point at which any real hope of a better life is extinguished.

Even as we encourage this kind of multidimensional, community-based approach to investing in American youth, one area calls out for immediate attention—the vital need to rid our youth of the plague of drug and alcohol addiction. Although we have no easy answers, **we recommend that drug and alcohol treatment on demand be made a reality in this country, not just for youths, but for all Americans.** We have generally avoided recommending new entitlement programs in this report, **but one entitlement we do need is the guarantee of help in overcoming addiction for all who seek it. We also recommend further research, demonstrations, and evaluations of innovative programs to help solve this critical problem.**

Reducing School Dropout Rates ✓

Dropping out of school is typically a direct route into unemployment or at best an unskilled job with little potential for growth or real security. One study has found that more than one-quarter of male dropouts and nearly one-third of female dropouts are without jobs, and of those working, only a small fraction have skilled jobs. Teenagers quit school for a variety of reasons: lack of interest and motivation, family problems, peer pressure, the lack of positive role models, disgust with bad schools and teachers, poor self-esteem, academic failure.

Reducing the school dropout rate requires a blending of programs that attempt both to improve schools and stimulate individual students who are at risk of failure. Success hinges on making better opportunities available to young adults, increasing their awareness of these opportunities, and providing clear incentives for them to seize the opportunities. In short, there must be real and personal rather than bureaucratic and impersonal reasons to stay in school.

Today's most promising dropout-prevention programs are characterized by concerted action aimed at expanding the life options of disadvantaged youngsters. This is achieved in several different ways. It is too early to prove scientifically which of the current efforts are effective, but the early returns are generally positive. **Communities across the country need to learn from these programs and develop their own set of coordinated actions.** The general types of programs are briefly outlined below.

Educational Incentives for Youth. Some programs are attacking the school dropout problem directly by offering personal incentives to remain in school. They are usually funded by contributions from businesses, wealthy individuals, or universities.

Incentive Programs to Keep Students in School

Students graduating from East Harlem's Public School 121 (an elementary school) will receive college tuition if they complete the next six years of school and graduate from high school. This program, started by businessman Eugene Lang, also features counseling, student activities, and more student decision making. The program led to the establishment of the "I Have a Dream" Foundation that is helping about twenty other cities form such programs. In January 1988 New York Governor Mario Cuomo proposed a new statewide Liberty Scholarship Fund modeled along the lines of the Lang incentive program and made a public commitment to halve New York's dropout rate during the next five years.

The city of Cleveland is experimenting this year with a new program placing college tuition grants aside for students who achieve specific grades in high school. In Cincinnati, the Kroger Company has launched the Partnership in Education program with the Washington Park Elementary School. Students receive financial awards from the company for good attendance, good grades, and staying in school. The funds are applied to college tuition.

The importance of these investments lies in their ability to signal opportunity and to stimulate continuing efforts by saying to teenagers that somebody cares whether they finish school. The message is clear: "If you exert the effort to stay in school, maintain regular attendance, and get decent grades, we will see to it that your effort pays off." This type of deal links individual and social responsibility so that opportunity is created—but it must also be earned.

School-Based Reforms. New programs are developing to improve schools by decentralizing decision making so that it takes place at the level of the individual school. Principals and teachers are allowed more autonomy and independence, and teachers are given greater freedom to develop innovative programs for students in and outside the classroom. For example, in Florida's Dade County, twenty elementary, middle, and secondary schools and nine "magnet" schools—which draw students from a broad region into one school on a competitive basis—are participating in a new four-year project in decentralized, school-based management. This experiment features a curriculum geared to individual student needs, budget decentralization, and an enlarged role for collegial teacher decision making at the local school level.

Some communities are making teachers more accountable for their performance and connecting performance to career ladders. These new approaches try to break away from the top-down, bureaucratic control of large public school systems. It is important to chip away at the stifling rigidity and inertia of many school systems. It is equally important to reassert the once controversial but increasingly accepted notion that there are good schools and bad schools. Parents and officials need to pressure the bad schools to improve, and to reward that improvement when it occurs.

Collaborations Between Schools and Businesses

There are also encouraging signs that the business community is taking a more active interest in the quality of public schools. Schools and businesses share an interest in preparing young adults to hold jobs in today's economy. In recent years, their common concerns about the quality of schools and the quality of new workers have led to a wave of collaborative endeavors. A United States Department of Education survey of 9,000 school districts in 1984 showed that 22 percent had one or more active school-business partnerships. Most of these are "adopt-a-school" activities undertaken by local businesses, but some involvements are much more extensive.

School-business collaborations alone cannot revitalize depressed schools and school systems. Change must be anchored in the educational system itself—broadly defined to include teachers, administrators, community leaders, and concerned parents. However, the business community can become a powerful catalyst for improvement. The number of systematic, sustained efforts by business is growing, although much more needs to be done to focus school-business partnerships on serving the most at-risk, disadvantaged youths.

Educational Efforts Sponsored by Businesses

In Lawndale, Illinois, Chicago business leaders are developing a new privately funded school. Founder Joseph Kellman, president of Globe Glass and Mirror Company, has initiated Corporate/Community Schools of America, a group that proposes to open business-directed schools in other cities if the Chicago experiment proves successful.

Other initiatives funded or sponsored by businesses include Rich's Academy in Atlanta, an alternative high school for dropouts and low achievers who cannot function in a regular school setting; John Hancock Company's program to provide a range of services to English High School in Boston, including tutoring, career counseling and school renovation; and Honeywell's effort to tutor minority students who are having academic difficulty in the Virginia suburbs of Washington, D.C.

The Valued Youth Partnership program in San Antonio, cosponsored by Coca-Cola and the Intercultural Development Research Association, identifies high-risk students as "valued youth" and gives them an opportunity to serve as tutors of younger children. Since the program was implemented, absenteeism has declined; the dropout rate is lower; and the student tutors' grades, self-image, and behavior have improved.

The evidence suggests that serious school-business partnerships have achieved some modest success in their efforts to increase school attendance, reduce dropout rates, and improve academic performance. In its initial years the Boston Compact has witnessed a 6 percentage-point increase in the high school attendance rate, a 14-point increase in those city schools with the worst attendance rates, and substantial districtwide improvements in reading and math skills. However, the unchanging 43 percent high school dropout rate has led the compact to devise new strategies. The Philadelphia Academies, which deal exclusively with disadvantaged students, have achieved attendance rates that exceed 90 percent and high school graduation rates of approximately 80 percent. These are substantially ahead of the districtwide high school average (75 percent and 67 percent, respectively).

All of these programs illustrate the importance of self-esteem and a sense of purpose in achieving academic success, especially for those youths who already are not doing very well in life and who usually lack individual teacher attention and additional school support services. Business-school partnerships cannot work miracles but they can add an important impetus to school reform. Many public schools can also do much better by combining an emphasis on the life goals of disadvantaged students with mentoring, counseling, and a more innovative approach to the curriculum. Alternative schools may best draw out the abilities of students who are more deeply estranged from the existing educational system. **Various combinations of school reforms and business partnerships should be pursued to ensure that we do not give up on disadvantaged youths**.

Partnerships Between Schools and Businesses

A recent national survey highlights nine school-business partnerships that are being seriously pursued.

The most well-known is the Boston Compact, begun in 1982. The compact is an example of a partnership aimed at a citywide school system, rather than a business-to-single-school relationship. It represents an ongoing agreement between business, education, and community leaders that specifies particular hiring goals for business in exchange for measures of educational improvement in the city schools. The program is based on summer jobs, apprenticeship programs, scholarships for post-secondary education, and other help with the post high school transition. Special programs include younger, dropout-prone students, but the bulk of the efforts are directed toward older youths. Recently the National Alliance of Business has provided seed grants to seven other communities to facilitate the transfer of lessons from the Boston Compact. Other localities experimenting with partnerships focused on entire school systems include the Atlanta Partnership of Business and Education, the Invest Indianapolis Compact embracing the city and surrounding county, and California's statewide Regional and Occupational Centers and Programs.

Other partnerships are more student-focused in the sense of serving smaller groups of carefully targeted youths, usually with special classes and part-time jobs outside the traditional high school curriculum. The New Horizons program started in Richmond in 1980 and the Teen Opportunities program begun in Birmingham in 1981 are examples. The Philadelphia High School Academies program is unique in that it serves disadvantaged students during all four years of high school.

The four Philadelphia Academies (Business, Electrical, Automotive, and Health) offer a structured curriculum with few electives and an emphasis on both basic skills and vocational training, together with work experience in the junior and senior years. The academies are housed in ten comprehensive high schools and enroll 1,200 to 1,500 students. Academy students are drawn from those with low academic achievement records, test scores in the twentieth to fiftieth percentile within the district, and moderate to good school attendance records in the past. More than 100 city businesses are involved, providing substantial financial support, job placements, and advice on curriculum and program development.

Integrating Remedial Education, Work Experience, and Life Options Services. A number of models are emerging across the country that combine remedial education with part-time work and other services. Some programs focus on helping dropouts return to school or obtain graduate equivalency certificates. Other efforts are geared more to helping disadvantaged, non-college-bound students make a successful transition from school to work. In a variety of sites, experience is revealing effective strategies for action. The most promising programs offer a combination of services and have a centrally placed, core leadership that is responsible for setting clear standards, adopting methods that have been tested by experience, training staff on-site, and maintaining quality control.

The Summer Training and Education Program (STEP). This is a successful attempt to weave remedial education together with other necessary services. Although advantaged and disadvantaged children learn at about the same rate during the school year, the skills of disadvantaged children erode during the summer. Advantaged children generally score higher on standardized tests at the end of summer than they did at the beginning, but low-income children fall farther and farther behind, as home and peer influences often displace learning gains achieved in the school year. STEP is designed to stem the "summer learning loss" phenomenon by combining work, education, and counseling.

The STEP experiment has shown better results in each of its three years. In the summer of 1985 the first group of approximately 1,500 participants outscored the control group in both reading and mathematics by about one-quarter of a grade equivalent. Although that was progress, it was not enough to counteract summer learning losses entirely. By 1986, the first year of a two-summer involvement with the second group, STEP was able to stem the learning-loss phenomenon completely. Indeed, STEP's results with the second cohort were more than double those of the first. Most of the learning loss was avoided in reading, and in math participants registered a small gain over the summer. By the third summer, participants achieved a net gain in the level of their academic skills that was equivalent to one-half a grade level, more than gains experienced by similarly disadvantaged youth who were not in the program. Moreover, the program has had positive results with both black and Hispanic youths.

Although results are preliminary, it seems quite possible that by simply avoiding the learning losses that would otherwise occur in two or three summers of ado-

---

STEP: A Summer Project

STEP is a five-site demonstration project (Boston, Massachusetts; San Diego and Fresno, California; Seattle, Washington; Portland, Oregon) sponsored by Public/Private Ventures. It is operated jointly by school officials and employment and training personnel and paid for through the Federally funded summer jobs program.

During the summer, STEP offers fourteen- and fifteen-year-olds who are behind in school half days of work experience, half days of intensive and individualized remedial education, and a series of counseling sessions concerned with "life planning." The latter sessions seek to show the connections between the cost of raising a family, the kinds of jobs needed to support a family, the education necessary to obtain such jobs, and the effect of early pregnancy on life goals.

The project began operations in 1985 and has functioned for three summers. Participating schools normally provide academic credit for gains made during the summer and offer follow-up activities to help participants sustain these gains during the next school year.

The Comprehensive Competencies Program (CCP)

Developed by the Remediation and Training Institute, CCP is a self-paced learning program that maximizes the amount of time students spend on clearly specified learning tasks as well as the amount of time teachers can spend with individual students. Its educational materials are based on approaches that have been proven through research to be effective in reaching disadvantaged individuals. This curriculum is combined with the business world's technique of franchising to ensure efficient delivery of uniformly high-quality-services.

CCP is now being used in 250 learning centers by a variety of community-based organizations, private industry groups, secondary and postsecondary institutions, and it reaches 30,000 teenagers and adults annually. The CCP program uses a comprehensive array of instructional techniques, including computer exercises, workbooks, audiovisual devices, supplementary readings, and personal teacher assistance. A new English-as-a Second-Language (ESL) program is currently being disseminated in the system. Most organizations combine CCP with other training and work experience.

---

lescence, disadvantaged students could pick up at least one grade level and reduce the amount of time teachers must spend reteaching what has been forgotten between school years. STEP also appears to be having strong positive effects on sexual knowledge, attitudes and behavior—thereby reducing pregnancy rates among fourteen- to sixteen-year-old girls.

A persistent problem in many efforts to keep disadvantaged youth in the mainstream has been a lack of sustained good management and quality control in the various programs. Too often, decentralization has translated into failure to use techniques of remedial instruction that have proven effective. The Comprehensive Competencies Program (CCP) is a valuable illustration of how local initiative can be combined with business efficiency and professional educational competence. CCP provides quality remedial education materials and support services to a wide variety of local groups, using techniques that have been proven effective by social science research.

The results show that disadvantaged students with multiple problems and a record of failure in other settings can achieve significant learning gains. CCP enrollees include many dropouts, single parents, delinquents, welfare recipients, and members of minority groups. During twenty-eight hours of total instruction time they gain an average of one grade level in reading and 1.4 grades in mathematics. Impressive results also have been shown with a newly developed program for Hispanics with a limited knowledge of English.

Teenagers who are headed neither for college nor for a clear vocation are too often neglected. Although they will soon be leaving school, they generally receive

JAG for High School Seniors

JAG began in the state of Delaware in the late 1970s, and since then has expanded its operations to thirteen states serving 12,000 students annually in more than 275 high schools. The JAG Board of Directors is made up of state governors, education commissioners, business CEOs, and labor leaders. Emphasis is placed on creating statewide school-to-work transition programs and drawing upon the leadership of governors and state commissioners of education and labor. Six state legislatures currently provide special appropriations to support JAG.

Each local JAG program targets high school seniors who are identified by school officials and JAG staff as being most at risk of dropping out or becoming unemployed after graduation. These are usually general education students who have not enrolled in college preparatory or vocational education courses, who have little employment experience, and whose grades are average or below average.

Most classes are offered as an integral part of the school day. JAG offers a curriculum and testing system that requires the mastery of twenty-nine employment-related competencies. It is based in part on CCP materials. In addition to a common curriculum, each local JAG program provides career counseling, instruction in employment competency, job placement services, and nine months of follow-up services after graduation.

little if any instruction about the world of work, career options, or job-search techniques. High school counselors and others in the educational system usually spend little time with them. Jobs for America's Graduates (JAG) tries to fill this gap. It is probably the largest school-to-work transition program for non-college-bound youths, and it is certainly the largest to gain the support of state governments.

JAG is a formal school-to-work transition program that seeks to link work at school with work in the labor market. Research has shown that the ultimate success of the program depends on the amount and the quality of time that a job counselor spends with each student. Often these counselors not only help with career planning and direct job placement but also coordinate special educational help for those students who have low basic skills.

Evidence for the success of the program has accumulated during the last eight years. When JAG participants are compared with a control group, the JAG students have more consistent work records, are twice as likely to be employed (72 percent vs. 36 percent), earn 25 percent higher wages, and gain greater increases in their incomes—20 percent annually and more than 50 percent for minorities. Overall, those benefiting from JAG are 86 percent more likely to be working full time after high school graduation than comparable groups. The results appear strongest for seniors who are most at risk of failing to make the transition from school to work—minorities, those who have never worked before, those from welfare families, and those who have a record of low achievement in school.

Reducing the Number of Teen Pregnancies

No discussion of the problems of young adulthood can be complete without considering teen parenthood. More than one million teenage girls become pregnant each year in the United States, and nearly 470,000 give birth. Teenage pregnancy rates in the United States are significantly higher than in most other industrial countries. It is particularly disturbing that U.S. girls *under* age fifteen are five times more likely to give birth than young adolescents in any other developed country for which data are available.

Generally speaking, the fact that mothers are teenagers tends to dampen the life prospects of both the mothers and their children. There is evidence that, compared with those who have their children later, early childbearers are much more likely to experience economic hardship and family disruption in later life, to drop out of school, and to fail to find stable and remunerative employment. An increasing proportion of teenage mothers are becoming welfare recipients under the Aid to Families with Dependent Children (AFDC) program. Moreover, these unmarried young mothers and their children make up the bulk of those who stay on the welfare rolls for extended periods. In 1985 welfare, Medicaid, and Food Stamp costs for families begun by births to teenagers were $16.65 billion.

Although early motherhood clearly affects chances for the socioeconomic success of young women, it by no means dictates the results. A recent study by sociologist Frank Furstenberg tracked teenage mothers for seventeen years in Baltimore, revealing that the best word to describe the subsequent life patterns of teenage mothers is "diverse." These women follow several different paths to recovery from the initial setback to economic self-sufficiency that results from early motherhood. About half eventually make it into the middle class as adults.

Furstenberg's study also found that informal support networks, parental support, and role models were very important elements in teenage mothers' achieving economic independence. Other factors that work in a mother's favor are strong motivation and self-image and staying in or returning to school. Indeed, decisions to complete high school and to postpone additional births are crucial. According to Furstenberg's study, programs such as that of Baltimore's Poe Alternative School and Sinai Hospital, which offer comprehensive medical and social services to improve prenatal and neonatal care, are successful in changing behavior (e.g., using contraception) in ways that increase the mothers' likelihood of staying in school and postponing further pregnancies.

For many young women in the United States, the delivery of a first child leads to their first contact with the social welfare system. If that system provides immediate health-care services and helps a young mother learn parenting and job skills, there is every reason to hope that she and her child can become self-sufficient and comfortable.

This evidence from Furstenberg's study indicates that staying in school, getting a job, and developing skills *can* make a difference for young mothers—even if they are temporarily trapped in a cycle of poverty and dependency. The "children of children" may face tough odds, but they are not doomed to failure, and their prospects for success hinge not only on their own ability, but also on the degree to which their mothers are helped to overcome the disadvantages of early parenthood. Studies have shown that family background—above all, the educational attainment of the mother—is a crucial determinant of a child's life chances. Clearly mother and child must be helped together, with equal priority given education and remedial help for the parent and the child.

At the same time, local program operators report that, in comparison with twenty years ago, they are now having to deal with a much more difficult group of troubled teenagers who are experiencing multiple problems, are without family supports, and are often caught up in drugs. Any realistic approach must acknowledge that teenage pregnancy is not a self-contained "problem" but part of a complicated pattern of personal and social disarray. If all pregnant teenagers suddenly became married or if their pregnancies miraculously disappeared, we would still be left with the same millions of young people—both girls and the boys they could potentially marry—who are lacking a basic education, are ill-equipped to function in the modern labor market, and are otherwise unprepared for adult responsibilities.

Unfortunately, attention to the real problem is too often obscured by a fruitless debate between those who claim that information, counseling, and contraceptives are the answer and those who contend that these measures simply encourage sexual activity among teenagers, who would benefit from instruction on abstinence and moral values. There is much reason to believe that a successful effort to reduce the number of teenage pregnancies will require both increased knowledge about the consequences of sexual activity and greater personal motivation to use that knowledge in realistic, constructive planning for the future.

The most successful school clinic programs are not simply contraceptive dispensaries, but also offer comprehensive health care, counseling, and education for adolescents. The number of school-based clinics has grown rapidly in the last few years, totaling 124 schools in thirty states by 1988. Although research results are preliminary and more evaluations need to be done, there is good evidence from some sites, particularly St. Paul and Baltimore, that school-based, comprehensive health-care programs do reduce the incidence of pregnancy in teenagers. Similarly, major studies of teen pregnancy make it clear that sex education must encompass more than just information about sex or contraceptives. It must extend to the attitudes, motivation, and behavior of boys as well as girls. Amid the pressures of peers and the media, young people should be taught to think clearly about personal sexual behavior and the relevance of pregnancy to the achievement of personal educational and occupational goals.

New, realistic programs to help reduce the number of pregnant teenagers include: peer counseling to encourage teenagers to postpone sexual activity; community-based and school-based clinics that offer health-care services and counseling on the use of contraceptives; family life and sex-education programs; and enhancement of self-esteem through athletic activities and the performing arts. One such program is the Multi-Service Family Life and Sex Education program in New York City. This project helps about 150 adolescents and their parents with counseling sessions, educational assistance, and job experience. An experimental three-year project began in 1988 on Chicago's South Side and in Newark and Camden, New Jersey, focuses on teenage parents who are already on the welfare rolls. This Teenage Parent Demonstration emphasizes not only the obligation of such young people to work toward their economic self-sufficiency, but also the public assistance system's responsibility to provide services and support. Case managers help participants fulfill plans for continued education, skills training, and work experience. These efforts are linked to child care, medical services, parenting education, family-planning workshops, and housing assistance. The program also seeks to enforce child support from absent fathers by establishing paternity, acquiring support awards, and offering job-search and placement services to fathers. Teenage parents are part of the larger body of families that need active support in caring for children. Although especially vulnerable, they are but one more example of a situation in which social welfare policies must improve parents' ability to care for their children, rather than waiting until childrearing failures compound the problems. Programs such as Maryland's Family Support Initiative (discussed in Chapter Two) are particularly relevant to the problems of pregnant teenagers.

It is vitally important to develop a two-part strategy. The first part would encourage teenagers not to become pregnant. The second would help teenagers who do become parents to return to school while learning how to be good parents and providers. Programs featuring services to teenage mothers—ranging from counseling on nutrition and health to day-care services in the public schools—need to be designed to help avoid welfare dependency and keep young mothers in the mainstream of society. We must provide these services even as we encourage

fathers to contribute to their children's upbringing and—through education, training, and employment—help put them in a position to experience the benefits as well as the responsibilities of two-parent families.

Coordinating Efforts

The examples cited in this chapter carry an important message: We ought to invest in human capital with the same entrepreneurial spirit and concern for long-range payoffs that venture capitalists bring to investments in new enterprises. No sensible investor expects every initiative to succeed or every investment to pan out. But if we are to have a viable economy and society, we simply cannot afford to write off a major chunk of the coming adult generation.

Clearly, we must also bring better management techniques and quality control to efforts aimed at preparing youth for the world of work. At present, responsibility for addressing needs among the huge and growing number of young people who lack the educational and occupational skills that are required to become productive citizens is—to put it mildly—unfocused. The tendency has been to isolate self-contained "problems"—educational deficiency, teen pregnancy, joblessness, family disorders, and so on—then to fund isolated programs run by self-contained agencies. As a result, efforts to deal with adolescents at risk of failure are typically piecemeal, dominated by short time frames, inadequately funded, and uncoordinated. A realistic policy is possible, but Federal, state, and local levels of government should be responsible for coordinating the various programs.

Efforts to help disadvantaged adolescents may draw upon many Federal programs, including the Job Training Partnership Act (JTPA), the Job Corps, summer jobs programs, Chapter 1 of the 1981 Education Consolidation and Improvement Act, and the Magnet Schools Assistance Program. Chapter 1 offers funding for educational services to disadvantaged students and the handicapped. **Funding should be increased to restore the real value of previous commitments in the Chapter 1 program. The growth of private-sector initiatives and public-private partnerships is no excuse for failing to fund federal programs adequately. Far from being incompatible, a community-level approach and sustained national funding are necessary to each other. We believe that efforts to slash funding for Federal programs aiding disadvantaged adolescents should be resisted.**

State governments are potentially in an excellent position to advocate coordinated approaches and proven practices because they generally have the legal and regulatory powers to guide local programs in education, child-welfare services, juvenile justice, vocational education, and other areas. Unfortunately, apart from campaigns against alcohol and drug abuse, most state governments have not yet seized this leadership opportunity. Although no one should underestimate the political and bureaucratic obstacles to state-level action, these obstacles are not insurmountable. Such states as Oregon, California, and Massachusetts have launched important efforts that have improved the management and delivery of services to at-risk youth. Moreover, in the past decade many state governors have shown they can take the lead in promoting educational excellence.

Reforms have raised academic standards and graduation requirements all across the country. These worthwhile efforts, however, can easily have the unintended consequence of making it more difficult to find educational alternatives for young people who did not do well even at the lower standards. It is time for states to make a similar "quality" commitment to helping below-average students. Under existing law, state governments have some discretion over Federal money that could do much to energize and shape local creativity. JTPA allows states to use 6 percent of total JTPA funds for incentives and technical assistance and 8 percent to improve ties between job training and the educational system. Governors may designate local service delivery areas for job training, review local plans, and control 22 percent of their allocations of Federal job-training dollars. And under Chapter 1 of the 1981 Education Act, state governments have authority to write the rules for how these Federal funds are used to help educate disadvantaged students.

We recommend that state governors and legislatures use these and other opportunities to leverage local action in a concerted, sustained attack on the problems of young people who are at risk of failing to make the school-to-work transition. Drawing upon the experience of the few states already active in this area, **we recommend the creation of interagency state youth councils composed of senior officials from educational, job training, and human service agencies. Such councils should be charged with developing strategies to coordinate service delivery, share information, and maintain continuity and quality control in local programs for at-risk youth.**

Local communities must take prime responsibility for designing and coordinating better programs to prepare young people for the job market. Localities do, of course, differ, but the examples in this chapter illustrate the basic elements that are necessary for success. These elements include:

- the use of schools as centers for delivering integrated services to adolescents;

■ early detection and early interventions that forestall problems instead of merely reacting to them after the fact;

■ willingness to recognize the interrelated nature of such problems as leaving school, teen parenthood, unemployment, and welfare dependency;

■ positive incentives and life-option counseling, so that young people have personal reasons to succeed in school and work;

■ private-sector involvement in educational and employment programs, together with adequate funding of public-sector programs.

We recommend that every community consider establishing a committee composed of school, job training, and business representatives. Such a committee should be charged with assessing the state of the community's resources and opportunities for young people and developing an action plan to deal with the deficiencies.

Conclusion

The problems explored in this chapter are most concentrated in inner-city areas and among the poor, but they are certainly not confined to those areas or groups. The educational achievement of all young Americans has deteriorated in recent years. A depressingly high proportion finish high school only marginally literate and wholly unprepared for the labor markets of the future.

We have not discovered any sure bets or easy strategies for addressing the cluster of problems that include teen pregnancy, school dropout rates, and deficient basic skills. There are promising models in selected communities, but they cannot and should not be transformed overnight into national programs. What works in Baltimore may not work in Phoenix. Nevertheless, models can be emulated and adapted to varied local circumstances.

In a recent publication issued by this project*, Gordon Berlin and Andrew Sum offered a simple litmus test to gauge the need to invest in young people. "If your child were falling behind in school, would you think it important to get him or her

---

Toward A More Perfect Union: Basic Skills, Poor Families, and Our Economic Future by Gordon Berlin and Andrew Sum. Occasional Paper 3, Ford Foundation Project on Social Welfare and the American Future. New York: Ford Foundation, 1988.

extra academic help in the evenings, the weekends, and during the summer? If we as a nation want to begin improving our rate of real economic growth, restoring growth in real wages and real family incomes, and reducing poverty and disparities in the incomes of various racial and ethnic groups, we should do no less for all of our nation's children."

The initiatives we call for in this chapter do not rely heavily on new Federal spending programs. The single exception to this is our call for funding drug and alcohol abuse treatment for all who need to seek it; we have recommended that $1 billion be earmarked for that effort. This does not mean, however, that the ideas presented in this chapter carry no price tag. Many of the models we have described will require a commitment of community resources. States, cities, private businesses, and voluntary organizations will have to find new funds—and redeploy existing ones—to improve basic skills, help young people stay in school, and promote more successful transitions from school to work. If these efforts are to be effective, Federal programs *must* complement and support them.

Because it has not invested sufficiently in its youthful human capital, American society is now faced with a major salvage operation. An important part of the nation's future depends on the success of this effort.

Chapter Four

The Working Years:
Increasing Economic Opportunity
and Social Protection

The American ethos stresses the importance of pursuing individual opportunity through work. At the same time, work traditionally has enabled employed persons to weave sturdy safety nets that protect themselves and their families by a combination of government social insurance (Social Security and Medicare) and employer-provided benefits (private pensions, group health plans, and disability insurance).

There are two problems with this system: It excludes too many people, and it was designed long ago and needs a thorough overhaul. Approximately 2 million Americans work full time all year, while remaining below the official poverty line. When their children and other family members are included, some 6 million impoverished Americans live in family units in which someone works full time twelve months a year. This is a problem that affects single- and two-parent families alike. For example, during the past decade increases in the Hispanic poverty rate have been chiefly due to lower real incomes among Hispanic workers in two-parent families. About 24 million workers and their dependents risk personal financial disaster because they have no health insurance coverage whatsoever. Further, only about 30 percent of more than 6 million people who are unemployed receive any unemployment compensation; this is the lowest proportion in the program's fifty-year history.

Current policy puts too little emphasis on work opportunities. At the same time, it provides too little protection for those who are seeking work or working at low-paid jobs. Recently passed Federal welfare reform measures begin to move in the needed direction, but much more should be done to improve the incomes, opportunities, and social protections of American workers. We believe that creating an appropriate work-based response depends less on designing one big program and more on putting together many different components of social support for Americans during their working years.

Economic Growth: A Necessary but Not Sufficient Condition

Vigorous economic growth is not a panacea for all social problems, but it is an important precondition for achieving the goals presented in this report. Only a strong economy will generate a supply of jobs that complements much-needed investments in children and young people. A vigorous economy is also vital to the peculiarly American system of employment-related social welfare protection. To benefit from work-based "credits" and social insurance, one must first gain access to them. Providing sufficient access requires generating enough jobs for the working-age population.

There is a clear relationship between the pace of economic growth and the reduction of poverty rates. Slow growth during the 1973–83 decade increased poverty rates by 4.5 percentage points and reduced by about 20 percent the share of the total national income that the poorest fifth of the population received. A stagnant economy leaves our social welfare system with unmanageable "zero sum" choices. Any addition to the standard of living for one group must come from a reduction in the living standard of another group. Strong economic performance makes it much easier to meet one set of social needs without reneging on other commitments.

For all these reasons, a solid social welfare policy for the United States depends on a sound economy. Unfortunately, between 1973 and the mid-1980s the U.S. experienced higher than normal rates of unemployment, stagnant real wages per worker, and sluggish productivity. Annual productivity increases, which had averaged 3.3 percent between 1947 and 1965 and 2.5 percent between 1966 and 1973, slowed to less than one percent between 1974 and 1982. After rising throughout the postwar years, wages adjusted for inflation stopped growing and in some cases actually declined from 1973 through the mid-1980s.

Economic stagnation created greater inequality among Americans in terms of their lifetime prospects for material well-being. Following the early 1970s, fewer jobs paid enough for their holders to afford a middle-class standard of living. Those who had already attained such a standard often could not keep up, while those who had not attained it had to struggle harder and more often failed.

In the past two or three years there has been some improvement in economic conditions. Real output and productivity have grown at a brisk pace, and the depreciation of the U.S. dollar against the yen and several European currencies has helped spark a recovery in exports. Job growth has been substantial and unemployment is relatively low. Demographic forces portend tight labor markets in the future.

Yet during the past ten to fifteen years, the growth in real wages per worker has remained less robust than in the earlier postwar period. Furthermore, it has become increasingly apparent that even in tight labor markets, when the labor force is more or less fully employed, people with limited education and deficient basic skills continue to suffer. Indeed, the problem we face today is not so much slack demand or sluggish overall productivity as the number of new entrants into the labor force who are simply unqualified for work. That is why this report puts so much emphasis on education and training.

As earnings per worker have failed to increase very much since the early 1970s, the struggle to maintain living standards has taken several forms. The number of workers per household has increased. By 1985 more than half of all women of working age were in the labor force, compared with about 35 percent in 1944, which was the peak of World War II, a time when many women were drawn into the work force.

By delaying childbearing and having fewer children, Americans, on the average, have reduced the number of family members who must be supported by a single income. They have also been saving less and borrowing more to finance their consumption in the 1970s and 1980s. In the 1985–88 period, personal savings as a percentage of disposable income have been in the range of 3 percent to 5 percent. That compares with 5 percent to 9 percent during most of the postwar period. Similarly, in the late 1980s the United States switched from being a creditor to a debtor nation, annually borrowing from abroad sums equal to more than 3 percent of its gross national product. These funds have not been used to raise the level of investments but to cover huge Federal deficits and thus finance further domestic consumption.

Clearly, social and attitudinal changes, along with economic pressures, drive such long-range trends as the rise in female participation in the labor force, the decline in childbearing, and the reduction in savings. To some extent, however, these trends reflect adjustments made by American families to the squeeze on the real earnings of their primary breadwinners. These changes will not keep the proverbial wolf from the door forever. While the effects of economic stagnation may be postponed, they cannot be made to disappear. One cannot continue borrowing in order to consume and expect that the bills will never come due. The nation has already mortgaged a significant part of its future growth in the 1990s simply to service the debt it owed to foreign creditors in the 1980s.

The fact that the economy has picked up in the past couple of years is encouraging, but it is no cause for complacency. On the contrary, the current period, which has been characterized by tightening labor markets and continued employment gains, provides an excellent opportunity for action. Many of the recommendations offered here would be harder to accomplish in a slack economy with high unemployment.

This is not a report on economic policy as such; however, there is no escaping the fact that viable social policies must be built on a solid foundation of prudent economic management. This means facing up to some unpleasant but necessary realities: **The Federal deficit should be reduced through steps that achieve real long-term savings rather than one-time or illusory savings. Policy makers must be willing to make politically difficult changes in our entitlement programs, our discretionary non-defense programs, and our non-critical national defense outlays. Citizens must stand ready to provide the revenue necessary to finance national commitments.**

We are spending about $150 billion a year just on the interest on the Federal debt. This enormous cost of servicing our government's debt robs money that might be used for our vital social welfare needs. The mounting debt foists costs that we should be paying ourselves onto our children and grandchildren, and will hamper their capacity to meet their own needs down the road.

A more responsible fiscal policy will permit a more expansionary monetary policy, and this combination should help create jobs. Reducing the Federal debt will take some pressure off our meager private savings. But **we will still need to arrest the decline in savings and to increase our investments. This means that consumption will have to grow more slowly.**

Productivity growth will be facilitated by an increase in saving and investment. **We also need to enhance productivity through flexible compensation, incentive pay, and profit-sharing arrangements, along with reforms in obsolete work rules. Measures that allow workers to change jobs without losing pension and health benefits would also foster the kind of flexibility and mobility that we need if our labor force is to become more competitive.**

Improving the Return on Work

In the long run, if young people receive better education, training, and access to health and nutrition services, they will be better qualified for good jobs. But efforts on behalf of young people, outlined in the previous two chapters, have to be coupled with more immediate help to those who are already in their working years. At present many people work full time—or as much as they can, given their family responsibilities—and yet do not earn enough to support themselves or their families at society's minimal level.

One way of illustrating the situation is to look at the number who are working but remain below the official poverty line. Most of these people are employed part time or full time for only part of the year, but a significant minority—some 2 million persons with perhaps double that number of dependents—are working full time all year around. The jobs they hold are the most marginal in terms of employment, security, pay, benefits, and opportunities for advancement. As Figure 4.1 shows, the 1980s have seen the number of such workers with very weak purchasing power rising significantly in comparison with the 1970s.

Figure 4.1 Number of Persons Working Full Time Year-Round and Living Below the Poverty Line

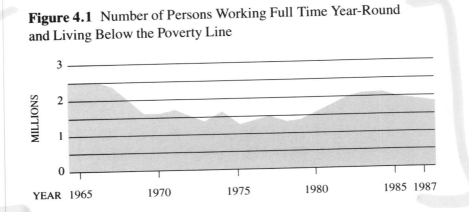

Source: U.S. Bureau of the Census. In *Working but Poor*, by Sar Levitan and Isaac Shapiro. Baltimore: Johns Hopkins University Press, 1987, p. 4.

There is no one simple policy that will neatly address the problems of the working poor, since they are a very diverse group. Even if we could afford it, few people would feel that we had dealt with the issue if we simply guaranteed everyone a minimum, poverty-line income through some combination of welfare reform, food stamps, and the like. Studies of low-income Americans' own preferences show that they have a very strong attachment to work, regardless of race, sex, ethnicity, or age. Their own hopes for bettering their lot lie with jobs, education, and training—not with government handouts. The jobs of poor women are particularly inadequate, with impoverishing pay, not enough hours, few employee benefits, and scant opportunities for advancement. A more meaningful response to the problems of the working poor would aim to improve the income and benefits that come from work and to recast the passive support system that tides people over when they are not working.

The minimum wage represents society's effort to establish a floor below which market forces will not be allowed to drive down the living standards of workers. Minimum-wage workers tend to be part-time employees (some of whom want full-time work) and women, including a disproportionately large share of female heads of families. About half of such workers are age twenty-five or older, and there is a historical tendency for wages of workers below the poverty line to cluster around the minimum wage level.

Since the beginning of 1981 the minimum wage has remained frozen at $3.35 an hour, and therefore its real value after inflation has declined sharply. As Figure 4.2 shows, it has become increasingly impossible to support a family even at the poverty line while working full time for the minimum wage. Economists have long debated the effects of minimum-wage legislation in deterring employers from hiring. There is evidence that suggests that an increase in the minimum wage has some adverse effects on the job prospects of teenagers and young adults, but the effects are relatively slight.

The earnings of today's lowest-paid workers must be undergirded by a higher minimum wage. **We recommend restoring the purchasing power of the minimum wage to its 1981 level**.

Even if we restore the purchasing power of the minimum wage, however, the standard of living afforded by a full-time job would not be sufficient to lift all families out of poverty if there was only one worker in the household. Although the minimum wage could be lifted still further, the potential impact on inflation and on employment opportunities for low-skilled workers would make this an unattractive option. Fortunately, we need not rely exclusively on the minimum wage to improve workers' earnings. There is a second tool, the Earned Income Tax Credit (EITC).

Started as a little-noticed amendment to the tax laws in 1975, the tax credit is set as a percentage of initial earnings and phased out as earnings rise. When the income taxes due are small or nonexistent (as they are for low-wage employees), the worker is refunded the difference between the tax liability and the size of the credit. The EITC is currently set at 14 percent of family earnings up to $6,200.

The wages paid a worker take no account of the number of family members dependent on that wage and neither, under current law, does the EITC. Thus a family consisting of two persons and with earnings of $7,000 a year receives the same credit in 1988 as a family of six—$868. If both of these families earn just enough to reach the poverty threshold for their respective family sizes, the two-person family will receive an EITC payment of $868, while the larger family with a higher poverty threshold receives only $239. This inequity occurs because the ceiling on the tax credit does not vary with family size, while family financial needs obviously do vary with family size.

Although labor markets cannot vary compensation in relation to family responsibilities, public policies can and should take account of the presence of dependents. Hardship is much greater among those workers struggling more or less permanently in the low-wage sectors of the economy and facing major responsibilities as breadwinners.

Figure 4.2 Value of Full-Time Work at the
Minimum Wage in Relation to the Official Poverty Line

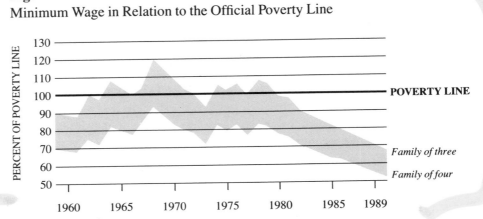

Source: U.S. Department of Labor. In *Working but Poor* by Sar Levitan and Isaac Shapiro. Baltimore: Johns Hopkins University Press, 1987, p. 52.

We recommend expanding the Earned Income Tax Credit by varying its benefits with the size of a recipient's family. A straightforward method of adjusting the EITC by family size would be to increase the credit rate according to the number of dependents. A 4 percentage-point increase for each additional dependent would add about $250 per additional dependent to the maximum size of the credit. Thus, the 14 percent rate that currently applies to all families would apply to a family with one dependent child, households with two dependent children would get an 18 percent tax credit, those with three children would get 22 percent, and families with four or more children would qualify for a 26 percent credit. In addition, better administrative procedures could be developed to refund EITC benefits on a regular advance basis rather than in a lump-sum payment at the end of the tax year.

Assuring Health-Care Coverage

An employee benefit package offers many important features, including employer contributions to pensions and disability insurance. The lack of basic health-care coverage, however, is a major problem. Assuring such coverage not only affords protection but also fosters opportunity and productivity by improving health, reducing the amount of time away from work, and keeping workers financially solvent.

At present an estimated 31 million to 37 million Americans have no health insurance coverage. Many others have coverage, but their insurance does not provide protection against the major expenses of catastrophic illnesses. The large number of uninsured people in the United States results from significant gaps in the two major systems that cover the working-age and young population: Medicaid and employer-provided group health insurance. About 24 million people—or two-thirds of the uninsured—are either full-time workers or their dependents. Medicaid, a Federal-state program, now covers fewer than half of the poor. Thus, aside from the elderly, at least one in six Americans falls into a deep chasm between these two systems. Getting into the work-based health insurance system requires having the right kind of job. Jobs in certain industries or occupations do not typically provide coverage, nor does the part-time work that now accounts for one of every six jobs.

Eligibility for Medicaid varies from state to state. In general, families headed by a working adult find it very difficult to qualify, even when the worker earns the minimum wage and household income is well below the poverty line. These workers' incomes are too low to achieve a decent living standard, but too high to allow them to qualify for Medicaid in many areas of the country. Their jobs often do not provide private health insurance.

In the past, many of the people who were uninsured had their health-care costs paid for by the "hidden tax" of cost shifting. Doctors and hospitals increased their bills to paying patients to offset the costs of treating the uninsured. Today, this cost shifting to cover uncompensated care is becoming more difficult. Large employers are bargaining more aggressively with service providers, either indirectly through their insurance carriers or directly as self-insured purchasers. Meanwhile, cutbacks in government financial support for community health centers and the National Health Service Corps, as well as new limits on Medicaid services and eligibility, have further eroded health services to the indigent.

These changes affect the willingness of doctors, hospitals, and other providers to treat the uninsured—poor and nonpoor alike. To be uninsured in America today is to be more vulnerable to exclusion from the health-care system. The challenge is to replace the eroding and inefficient cross-subsidies with new, more direct ways of paying for those with limited access to coverage.

The national goal should be universal health coverage for all Americans. To achieve it, we recommend a blend of private-sector initiatives and public-sector reforms. The answer to this problem is not simply to qualify for Medicaid all of those currently lacking insurance. This would give some businesses an incentive to drop coverage, and it would solidify the questionable link between welfare and health insurance. At the same time, if we rely solely on voluntary employer initiatives to expand private coverage, the results are likely to fall short. Many employers find health coverage too expensive and cannot or will not provide it on their own. A requirement that all workers be given a full package of benefits may lead to significant job losses, particularly for lower-paid workers, many of whom have only a tenuous attachment to the labor force, working a few weeks a year or a few hours a week.

It is realistic and fair to insist that the private sector assure basic health protection for those workers with a strong, permanent attachment to the labor force. Indeed, assuring people who take a job and stick with it for a significant period of time that they will have private health insurance enhances the attractiveness of work and diminishes the appeal of welfare dependency.

We recommend a new approach that requires employers either to offer a basic package of health insurance coverage to workers (that includes catastrophic expense coverage) or to contribute an amount per employee to a public fund that will finance coverage for uninsured workers.

Eligibility would be restricted to workers with established job tenure (e.g., a certain number of hours worked in the first three months of a job) and to those working some minimum number of hours per week. The government guarantee should be adequate to purchase a certain minimum level of health benefits, but not so generous as to compete with employer-sponsored health plans.

With this approach, the private sector would take special responsibility for assuring coverage to a group with which it has a natural link—workers with a strong attachment to the labor force.

This strategy should be accompanied by a series of steps to assist those who are only marginally employed or who are unable to work for reasons of ill health or disability. These steps feature some basic reforms in our public assistance system:

- **We recommend that the Federal government extend the AFDC program to establish a minimum cash-benefit level that assures Medicaid eligibility to**

at least the poorest of the poor. (This will be discussed in more detail in the section on welfare later in this chapter.)

■ **Medicaid coverage should not be limited to those who receive cash welfare assistance.** Federal law now permits states to extend Medicaid to people who live below the poverty level but do not receive cash assistance; the new welfare reform law mandates a year's coverage for those who are just off the welfare rolls. Beyond this, special emphasis should be placed on extending Medicaid, without time limitations, to people who are poor, categorically ineligible for cash assistance, and not working enough hours or weeks to qualify for the mandated coverage specified above.

■ **Medicaid should place more emphasis on early treatment and preventive health care.**

Redesigning Unemployment and Welfare Programs

For people of working age, two basic components of the income-maintenance system are Unemployment Insurance (UI) and Aid to Families with Dependent Children (AFDC). Both were initiated in the mid-1930s under conditions that were very different from those of today. These programs should be fundamentally reoriented to reflect present economic and demographic circumstances.

Instead of enhancing employment opportunities and real social protection, both UI and AFDC have evolved into systems that too often involve no more than income maintenance. Neither program places enough emphasis on training and retraining people to develop skills that are needed in today's labor market. At the same time, both programs provide cash benefits that have eroded in real terms and that vary widely from region to region, so that benefits in some states are simply too low. Both programs should be redesigned to do the following: first, provide more adequate short-term income support for assistance between jobs and for training people for long-term participation in the labor market; and second, offer greater incentives for people to take a job after this up-front investment is made.

Unemployment Services. Although a growing economy is a prerequisite for ensuring opportunity to the working-age population, there will undoubtedly continue to be periods of economic recession and substantial unemployment. Furthermore, the continuous ebb and flow of economic activity across the nation means that some regions, states, and labor market areas will experience periods of significant unemployment even when the nation's overall economy is relatively healthy.

For the past half century, the unemployment compensation system has helped those with substantial work histories weather limited periods of joblessness. But as the economy and labor force have changed and the state unemployment insurance trust funds have been battered by recessions, the UI program has become a less adequate component of the safety net. In 1986 only one-third of the unemployed received UI benefits, and in some subsequent months the proportion has dropped to one-quarter. By contrast, during the 1970s about half of the unemployed received benefits, compared with more than 60 percent in Germany, Japan, and Sweden. Recent labor market entrants and many re-entrants do not receive benefits because they lack sufficient work histories, while others have exhausted their twenty-six weeks of coverage.

Unemployment Insurance was designed when adult males dominated the labor force and many of them worked at one job or one career all their lives. The system's goal was to tide such workers over during a layoff from a job to which they were likely to return when demand picked up. Today's work force is more diverse, and many laid-off workers will never return to their prior jobs. In a rapidly changing economy, more people will change occupations, industries, and regions in which they are employed. They still need some income maintenance. Even more important, they need new skills, retraining, or relocation assistance. Yet UI today continues to focus on income maintenance, not on changes in the labor market.

By becoming not just a safety net but more of a bridge, UI can help workers adapt to a changing, more global economy. Encouraging workers to adjust actively and positively to change is much preferable to retarding change. Workers who can "retool" their skills not only expand their opportunities, but also build a more lasting security than they could hope to acquire with the help of income maintenance policies.

A number of steps would reshape Unemployment Insurance to conform to the needs of tomorrow's unemployed workers. First, **we should tighten up administration of the program, particularly at the front end.** That means insisting that in order to qualify for benefits, new claimants who are unlikely to get their old jobs back quickly make a serious effort to obtain new jobs. In the past, only lip service has been paid to the "work test."

Second, **unemployed persons in declining labor markets should be able to receive their benefits as lump-sum payments that can be used to move to a more promising labor market.** Federal funds would appropriately be used to support this because the benefits of a more mobile labor market are truly national in scope.

Third, **we should recast the schedule of** UI **benefits so that they are high for the first few weeks, and then decline gradually as more training and employment services are provided**. This would substitute for the current system of constant-rate benefits that end abruptly after twenty-six weeks. The goal would be to combine better protection in the first few weeks, which are often critical to locating a new job, with stronger incentives to return to work. **Benefits for those who have experienced a long period of unemployment should be extended beyond the normal termination period only if the recipient agrees to participate in a serious retraining program**.

A declining-benefit approach would require the same total amount of money that is currently earmarked for UI. This idea is not proposed to save money, at least in the short run, but to create incentives for workers to return to work. Another option would be to pay the current level of benefits for thirteen of the first twenty-six weeks of unemployment, then phase down the level of the benefit over a period that might extend for another twenty to twenty-five weeks. In any case, it is important to recognize that there is nothing sacred about the current schedule simply because benefits have been paid at a constant rate for a specified time period since the program was started in the 1930s.

Finally, **solvency standards should be established to put the state unemployment systems on a sounder and more equal financial footing**. Although some states have done a great deal to restore the fiscal health of their systems during the past few years, many could not withstand even a mild recession. National, rather than state, revenue bases should be tapped to finance the extra costs that occur when the national unemployment rate is extremely high or when an individual state experiences an unemployment rate that is persistently above the national average. In addition, interstate differences in unemployment benefits are greater than can be justified by differences in the cost of living, and these disparities have not been shrinking. **These differences should be narrowed by increasing benefits in those states with particularly low benefit levels**.

In summary, we need to assure those who lose their jobs a decent standard of living while they are unemployed. We also need to structure unemployment compensation so that it encourages and facilitates a return to work.

Welfare Programs That Assure Adequate Incomes and Work. People who have little or no previous experience in the work force cannot use the unemployment compensation system as a safety net. For some, the AFDC welfare system fills this role.

For too many years social welfare reform in America has been defined almost exclusively in terms of "fixing" the AFDC program, with its misleading stereotypes of welfare queens, chiseling, and lifetime membership on the welfare rolls. Since policy makers have established a program that specifically sets apart families with children that are headed by women, and pays them welfare checks, it is not too surprising that the public is led to perceive "the welfare problem" as entirely a matter of unmarried women raising children at taxpayers' expense. The facts are that most female heads of families are not on AFDC, and of those who are, roughly half use welfare as a temporary source of emergency financial help and not as a permanent means of support. To be sure, there are major problems with AFDC, especially for recipients who are more or less permanently enmeshed in passive dependency. Yet AFDC is only one subordinate part—not the heart—of the social welfare challenge facing America.

The current AFDC system is woefully out of date in ways that are actually quite similar to those noted with regard to Unemployment Insurance. Benefits are inadequate and vary widely by state. Despite the revolution that has occurred in female labor-force participation since AFDC was enacted a half century ago, there is too little emphasis on employment prospects.

The Family Support Act of 1988 does begin to address this problem. Its central features include the creation of a Job Opportunities and Basic Skills (JOBS) training program for AFDC members. The new law features education and training, job search, health benefits, and child-care support for program enrollees in transition to work; limited work requirements for two-parent families; and increased enforcement of child-support payments. The new JOBS program, however, will affect only a portion of AFDC recipients in the next few years. In addition, with the exception of an extension of the Unemployed Parent program to all states, there are no provisions for more adequate benefit levels.

The AFDC program remains an anachronism today. To fit today's economic, demographic, and social circumstances, AFDC should be fundamentally overhauled to become a work readiness and support program, rather than a limitless income-maintenance program. For those on AFDC who can work, there is not enough opportunity or incentive to do so; for those who cannot work, or who are legitimately engaged in uncompensated activities such as the care of very young children, there is too little security because of inadequate payments and services. In short AFDC, like UI, lacks a realistic strategy for achieving both opportunity and security.

Much has been learned in recent years about the value of work in welfare programs. Experiments conducted by the Manpower Development Research Corporation (MDRC) suggest that welfare recipients generally accept programs combining job-search assistance, training, and work obligations. Such programs have led to worthwhile improvements in employment and income for single mothers on AFDC, as well as gradual reductions in their welfare dependency. The results of the MDRC research, together with other studies, do not reveal any dramatic "magic bullet." They do show that significant numbers of single parents on welfare can be helped to make the transition from welfare dependency to work.

Many states are now experimenting with new models of work and training that blend public help to the recipient, including day care and health coverage, with obligations to work. It has become clear that if they are to compete successfully in the marketplace, welfare recipients who have meager education and skills, little work experience, and have long been dependent on welfare require genuine, in-depth labor-market services (counseling, training, on-the-job experience, for example). This is something quite different from the pro forma, paperwork exercises that take place at too many state employment and welfare offices today.

At the same time, AFDC benefit levels are generally quite low, and there are huge discrepancies in the benefits offered by various states; maximum benefits for a family of four in California are five times as high as in Alabama. Participation in AFDC programs nationwide is limited by stringent asset tests that exclude all those with more than a token amount of resources or material possessions. Furthermore, little systematic effort is made to help those on welfare improve their employability and find a job.

We recommend that a national minimum benefit standard be established. No civilized country should tolerate benefit levels (AFDC plus Food Stamps) below half of the poverty threshold. **A national minimum benefit equal to two-thirds of the Federal poverty level (AFDC plus food stamps) is an achievable goal for the early 1990s.** In the long term, there is a need for more innovative approaches that expand employment opportunities. Raising benefits payments for those able to work makes sense only if cash assistance is used as a form of temporary support in emergency situations, not as a source of permanent income.

The welfare system should be overhauled to emphasize work instead of long-term dependency. Improving work readiness through education and training should be part of the new program. But an equally important part is making it clear to able-bodied healthy adults that welfare is time-limited—it will not go on forever. One way to accomplish this is to put a **limit on the length of time that those who can work are entitled to welfare benefits. This would be coupled with the provision of a public-sector job for those who have exhausted their benefits but cannot find work.** Government would, in effect, become the employer of last resort, providing jobs for those who cannot find work.

This approach would dramatically change today's welfare system, which is relatively cheap but open-ended. We would put more resources in at the front end, but make it clear that after some limited time period, welfare stops—and in its place comes work combined with other assistance such as day care. This would send a new message to people: "We will help you through a combination of support services and temporary welfare, which will be more generous than today's benefits, at least in many states with very low benefit levels. We will help make you job-ready with serious job-search assistance, training, health benefits, and temporary subsidies for child care or transportation. We will give you a reasonable time period to capitalize on this investment and land a job. After that, we will terminate benefits, but offer a backup public-sector job. Then, your choice will be between the job we offer and making it on your own, not between work and welfare."

Such a signal directly addresses the problem of persistent poverty and long-term welfare dependency. There are varying definitions of persistent poverty and the "underclass" in America. Estimates range widely from 2 million to 8 million people, but it is likely that no more than 10 percent to 15 percent of all poor people live in the poorest neighborhoods of our central cities. Substantial attention is paid to this problem in proportion to its size, because of serious social consequences that flow from concentrated destitution. A general absence of stable families, successful schools, and employed adults makes some inner-city neighborhoods breeding grounds for yet another generation of poverty and hopelessness. Into this already depressing setting, today's welfare system injects a message of passive maintenance and dependency. It is time to change that system and turn its signals toward work and personal responsibility.

No one should underestimate the challenge of providing useful public service jobs as a backup to welfare. Realistically speaking, many welfare recipients will not be able to find work, even with extensive job training and social support services. This will be particularly true for those in slack labor markets. America does not have much experience in running a national jobs program, and a smaller-scale public-service employment program was terminated in 1981. Developing a new one will require substantial resources and ingenuity.

In summary, the changes needed in AFDC are not so different from the reforms needed to refocus our larger social welfare system. The key terms are the same: investing in people, offering decent protection against insecurity, making opportunity real through work. In the case of AFDC this translates into a quid pro quo comparable to that for Unemployment Insurance. Government should offer people a greater front-end investment in employability and more adequate benefits for a reasonable period. In return, the recipient should be obliged to demonstrate a heightened sense of personal responsibility and a willingness to capitalize on the larger, but more time-limited public investment.

Our proposals aimed at helping working-age adults represent a mixture of new government spending and mandated changes in wages and employee benefits. These measures can touch the lives of individuals and families in a positive way, and thus indirectly improve circumstances in low-income communities. The major limitation of such reforms is that they are administered to individuals without directly addressing conditions in the neighborhood of which the individual is a part.

One effective way to deal with neighborhoods is to support community development corporations (CDCs). The Watts Labor Community Action Committee in Los Angeles, Chicanos Por La Causa in Phoenix, the Tacolcy Economic Development Corporation in Liberty City (Miami), and other CDCs make neighborhood-by-neighborhood improvements in housing conditions, street appearance, and safety. Concentrating on housing, commercial development, and the services that support these activities, such corporations provide an organizational structure for local community leaders to control capital, run social programs, and rekindle people's hopes. CDCs may promote street spruce-ups, neighborhood food shopping at fair prices, decent living space for the elderly, and recreational space for youth. They produce visible, tangible results that can provide power bases for community leaders and help attract new funds and residents to deteriorated neighborhoods.

The effect of community development corporations is to create an environment that signals renewal, not deterioration. Their efforts to change and improve communities are in step with the self-improvement efforts of individuals. Their success reinforces the values of the larger society. During the last two decades, several thousand development corporations have been created, along with several national organizations that fund and assist them with technical expertise. Thus, a system for expanding and strengthening them is already in place, a system that can absorb a significant infusion of new financing.

The problems of troubled neighborhoods are compounded by concentrations of the poor. At the same time, many low-, moderate-, and middle-income families find it increasingly difficult to acquire start-up homes or find housing at affordable rents. CDCs could play an important role in experiments that use tax incentives or tax credits to encourage the construction of low-, moderate-, and middle-income housing in troubled neighborhoods.

Community development corporations are only one important part of an effort to improve the environment in which people grow up and develop. We have also pointed out the need to rid our cities of crime and drugs and to rebuild their deteriorating infrastructure. Although our report concentrates on ways to build *human* capital, we are aware of the corresponding need to modernize our physical surroundings and improve the environment in which people can develop.

Estimating the Cost

Our proposals in this chapter have been aimed at helping adults by a combination of new government spending and mandated changes in wages and employee benefits. (See Figure 4.3 for a summary of the new government spending these proposals would require.) The estimates are the approximate costs of the reforms recommended in this chapter in the first year that they are fully implemented. These figures could vary for several reasons. For example, the estimated cost of a Federal floor on cash-assistance benefits ($3.7 billion) is predicated on our recommendation to set that floor so that the sum of AFDC and Food Stamp benefits equals 65 percent of the Federal poverty line (see Figure 4.3). Note that the estimated total cost of this step is a net figure that allows for the decline in Food Stamp outlays that would accompany an increase in AFDC benefits. It includes about $2 billion in new outlays by state governments, which share the cost of AFDC with the Federal government.

Figure 4.3 Summary of Government Outlay Increases for Programs to Help Working-Age Adults (First Year)

Program Initiative	Outlay Increase
Expansion of the EITC	$ 2.3 billion
Floor under AFDC benefits	3.7 billion
Expansion of Medicaid (adults)	3.0 billion
Retraining and UI reform	1.0 billion
Public-service jobs	2.0 billion
Total	$12.0 billion

The estimated cost of Medicaid expansion—$3 billion—is predicated on the coverage of adults who are poor, who lack both Medicaid and employer-sponsored group health insurance, and who would not be covered by the proposed mandated benefits program discussed in this chapter. (The cost of covering similarly situated poor children under Medicaid was included in the budget estimate in Chapter Two.)

An estimated 4 million adults would be covered by this expansion of Medicaid, and the cost estimate is predicated on a modest contribution by these beneficiaries of 10 percent of the actuarial cost of the Medicaid insurance.

A variety of programs can be devised for retraining or relocating displaced workers and for restructuring UI benefits. We think that a commitment of about $1 billion to this task, as was proposed in the 1987 budget deliberations, is a place to start if the money is spent in the ways outlined in this chapter.

It is hard to estimate the cost of providing public service jobs to those on welfare who cannot find a job after a specified period. It will depend on such factors as the time limit put on AFDC and the wage rate paid for these jobs. It will also vary with labor market conditions. The best time to try such an experiment is in a tight labor market like the one that is currently developing. We estimate a cost of $2 billion annually for this program.

The cost of the mandated health-care benefit package will depend upon its precise specifications. Initially imposed on employers, this cost could be partially shifted to workers in the form of lower employee compensation, or to consumers in the form of higher prices. To the extent that firms cannot shift the cost by adjustments in wages, prices, or dividends, they may try to find ways to produce goods and provide services with fewer workers.

The Congressional Budget Office has developed a cost estimate for one mandated health-care bill, S.1265, legislation that would affect 51 million people, 23 million of whom were previously uninsured, and that would add $27.1 billion in incremental costs to employment-based health plans. Of this total, $21.8 billion would come from employer contributions to new policies for workers who were previously uninsured, $3.3 billion from employee contributions to these policies, and $2 billion from new benefits that would be required under existing policies. The Congressional Budget Office has also estimated that $17 billion of this $27 billion price tag is money that is already being spent—directly or indirectly—on providing care to uninsured people. Such outlays include a portion of the cost of uncompensated medical care and a portion of the taxes paid to support the Medicaid program. Thus, the net cost of a mandated benefits approach—about $10 billion—is much less than the gross cost.

Chapter Five

Old Age:
A Time to Reap and
Sow Again

Public attitudes toward old age in America reflect two contradictory stereotypes. One portrays the elderly as needy, feeble, and dependent. A more recent caricature presents them as affluent, self-absorbed, and overindulged by taxpayers. The realities of old age are more complex, and the prevailing stereotypes serve mainly to distract attention from the real problems. Older citizens were once among the most destitute of Americans. Today the improved economic status of the elderly—resulting from a combination of public and private efforts (Social Security, Medicare, tax laws, personal savings, home ownership, and the like)—is a major success of U.S. social welfare policy.

Average per capita income for those older than 65 is now on a par with income per person in younger families, and the aggregate poverty rate for the elderly is below that of younger Americans. But there are huge disparities in resources and protection among the elderly. In 1984 only 7 percent of married couples sixty-five years of age or older lived in poverty, but 28 percent of white elderly single women were poor. For elderly single black women, the poverty rate was 62 percent. The poverty rate among the Hispanic elderly was 27 percent. Overall, about 12 to 13 percent of the elderly now live in poverty.

Social Security reforms in the past were designed to produce surplus reserves that would help ease the burden of paying for the large number of retiring baby boomers in the next century. However, these growing surpluses have not been treated as a form of national savings and investment to enhance economic growth—and thus to increase the resources needed in the coming retirement bulge. Instead, the Social Security surplus is being used simply to offset deficits elsewhere in the Federal budget. Meanwhile, Medicare, the national health insurance for the elderly, faces a mounting financial crisis. Current projections indicate that Medicare's Hospital Insurance trust fund will not be able to pay for current services shortly after the turn of the century. The day of reckoning could come even sooner if the experts' rather rosy assumptions about economic growth in the 1990s and the costs of the new Medicare catastrophic illness legislation are not borne out. In addition, large numbers of Americans are currently pauperized and emotionally drained by the expense of long-term care. As our population ages in the years ahead, the situation is only going to become worse. Yet we have not developed a workable public or private insurance approach to cope with the problem of long-term care.

In summary, the present system represents a paradoxical mixture of generosity and stinginess, huge spending and huge gaps. Few realize that the inequality of wealth is greater among the elderly than among other age groups. Moreover, the disparities in old age between the haves and the have-nots are likely to grow in the years ahead. This is because of the emerging difference between two groups: those depending almost exclusively on Social Security benefits that will grow more slowly than in the past, and those who will have profited from the escalating values of home ownership, from tax-favored savings initiated in the 1970s, and from expansions in private pension coverage that are most extensive for workers in higher-paying jobs.

Tragically, however, there is one great equalizer as Americans reach very old age and lose the physical or mental capacities to live independently. Only the extremely affluent will be able to pay for long-term care from their own resources. If we could look into the nursing homes of America, we would see, as we did in looking at infants through the nursery windows, the fundamental human vulnerability that we all ultimately share.

The basic theme of this chapter is straightforward: Some elderly Americans are not receiving enough help, while others are not contributing as much as they could. There is a growing mismatch between the vulnerability of old people and our social institutions that were designed to assuage it. Those elderly who can contribute more should do so—to help those who have been left behind, to help ensure a solvent Medicare system and a humane system of long-term care for themselves and others. New policies must not undermine the economic security and opportunity that have already been achieved for older citizens. But there are fair, progressive ways for the affluent elderly to help fill the gaps that exist in our social protection system, and we should not shrink from asking them to do so.

Protecting the Weakest Today

Older Americans have three lines of defense against economic hardship. First, almost all the elderly have access to Social Security and Medicare, two public social insurance programs to which people contribute throughout their working years. The poorest may claim income-tested benefits, mainly in the form of the Supplemental Security Income program, Medicaid, and Food Stamps. As a second line of defense, a significant number of Americans have private pensions and health insurance to complement Social Security and Medicare, although these "private" provisions are also publicly subsidized by favorable tax treatment. Finally, a much smaller minority of older Americans have financial assets that generate significant income to help meet expenses. This combination of supports meets the income needs of most older Americans quite well, but it still leaves too many in poverty.

Discussions of Social Security have a habit of concentrating on what will be happening ten, twenty, and even fifty years into the future. It is also important to remember income needs that are currently going unmet. Today, Social Security is the single most important source of retirement income for older Americans. If it were not for Social Security benefits, nearly half of our aged, rather than the current 12 percent, would live in poverty. In general, the lower one's income level, the more important Social Security becomes as a component of the household budget.

Currently about one-third of retirees have private pension income in addition to Social Security. Compared with those who are dependent solely on Social Security, these people are in a much better position to cover their expenses and stay within reach of their pre-retirement living standard. Those without a private pension are about four times as likely to live below the Federal poverty line as those with such pensions. In the years ahead, the number of retirees with private pensions will gradually increase, a trend reflecting the growth of employer-based pension coverage from the 1940s through the 1970s. Since the late 1970s, however, private pension coverage has declined moderately, and projections show employer-provided pensions will not be available to more than about one-half of the work force in the foreseeable future. For instance, of the unmarried women who will retire during the next five to fifteen years, almost two-thirds will lack private pensions. Overall, nearly half of today's workers receive employer contributions to a private pension, but a smaller proportion will actually see those pensions, in part because some workers still lose pension protection when they change jobs. Nevertheless, the proportion of people who will actually benefit is higher today than it used to be.

Although many older people possess some assets, few are able to derive significant income from them. Net wealth is much less evenly distributed than either income or private pension coverage, so that the richest 5 percent of the elderly account for well over half of all the net wealth of older Americans. About one-quarter of the elderly have no home equity, and many older citizens who are homeowners are understandably reluctant to re-mortgage their homes to generate income through reverse annuity mortgages.

In America today we see—or rather we too often fail to see—a large group of people who have little retirement income other than Social Security, and who, because of a limited earnings record, may find even that benefit to be minimal or nonexistent. They lack private pensions, and are in no position to gain either the current tax advantages or the long-range protection produced by salary-reduction plans, IRAs, Keogh plans, and the like. These destitute people are most likely to be living alone, to be very old, of minority race, and female. Single women represent almost two-thirds of the 3.5 million elderly persons living in poverty. Despite the rising living standards and economic security of the elderly in the aggregate, this large subgroup lacks adequate resources to meet basic housing, food, and health-care needs.

Many measures might have a long-term impact in helping the poorest of older Americans: an expansion of private pensions could be encouraged through tax breaks, for example, and reverse annuity mortgages could be made more accessible. Many poor would also eventually benefit from changes in long-term care. But one program can help destitute old people here and now. The Supplemental Security Income (SSI) program offers Federally financed cash benefits representing 77 percent of the poverty level for individuals (i.e., $4,032 a year in 1986) and 91 percent for couples. Somewhat fewer than half of SSI beneficiaries receive a very modest state supplement (median value in 1986 was $36 per month), and the real value of these supplements has declined by half since their initiation in the mid-1970s. About one-half of those eligible for SSI benefits do not even participate in the program. More than half of the elderly poor cannot get financial help with the unreimbursed costs of Medicare treatment because they are not on the SSI rolls and thus have trouble meeting Medicaid eligibility rules.

We recommend the following initiatives to improve basic income support for the impoverished aged:

- **an increase in Federal SSI benefits to assure minimum poverty-line incomes for those elderly without other sources of income;**

- **an easing of restrictive limits on liquid assets ($2,000 for individuals and $3,000 for couples in 1989) in order to qualify for SSI;**

- **a more effective outreach program to increase participation among those eligible for SSI.**

Protecting the Many Tomorrow

Social Security is likely to provide a basic minimum income for most Americans who retire in the future. Contrary to some popular impressions, the main danger in the years to come is not that the system will go broke. It is that the Federal government will consume the financial surplus that should be accumulating toward the day some twenty-five years from now when the unusually large baby-boom generation begins to retire.

The Social Security amendments of 1983 averted a crisis in the program and were also designed to set Social Security on a sustainable long-term path. The reforms reflected a roughly even split between tax and benefit changes. Scheduled payroll tax increases were accelerated, a portion of benefits above certain income levels was taxed for the first time, and the normal retirement age was raised starting in the early part of the next century and reaching age sixty-seven in the year 2022.

With these changes—and with moderate assumptions about economic growth, mortality, and fertility—the Social Security system should be healthy for the next fifty years. Of course, it is possible that weaker economic growth and smaller increases in productivity and real wages could produce trouble in the next century. Even should these possibilities occur, however, the solvency of the Social Security system could be maintained without Draconian measures. It is difficult to imagine a future in which a payroll tax increase of about 1 to 1 1/2 percentage points would fail to remedy any revenue shortfall. Such a tax increase would probably have some adverse effects on employment, but its impact would certainly be no greater than that of the payroll tax increases we have weathered in the last several decades.

The real problem to be faced in Social Security financing is not actuarial but political. The 1983 reforms were deliberately and prudently designed to accumulate a surplus that could be drawn on gradually to relieve the cost burden that will occur when the unusually large cohort of baby boomers begins retiring in the next century. The balance in the Old Age, Survivors' and Disability Insurance (OASDI) trust fund, which is the source of benefit payments to eligible retirees, must grow now to avert a deficit later (see Figure 5.1). The balance in the OASDI trust fund, which was $109 billion in 1988, will likely triple to $352 billion in 1997, and could grow to trillions of dollars during the next two or three decades. These surpluses represent necessary accumulations for the long-range solvency of the system.

The more immediate danger is that the growing balance in the Social Security trust fund will be diverted in ways that remove these funds from the pool of savings and put them into current consumption. Every politician can develop a laundry list of new spending initiatives, or bailouts for old programs, that could be funded from the surplus.

We recommend that the Social Security surpluses be saved and invested, not spent for consumption of current services.

Rescuing Medicare

Although Social Security has achieved a delicate financial balance over the long term, Medicare is headed for financial trouble in the near future. Current projections indicate that the Hospital Insurance trust fund of Medicare will be exhausted in the early part of the next century; a weaker-than-expected economic performance would hasten the day of reckoning, as would health-care costs that grow more rapidly than anticipated. (See Figure 5.1 for a graphic depiction of the difference between the Medicare and Social Security situations.) The Hospital Insurance trust fund that covers Part A, or the hospital part, of Medicare will gradually build a somewhat large balance in the next several years, and then quickly become exhausted about fifteen years from now. By contrast, the OASDI fund will accumulate huge positive balances that dwarf the size of the very temporary positive balances in the Medicare fund.

The Medicare health insurance system, a vital source of protection for tens of millions of older Americans, must be kept solvent. In 1989 legislation enacted by Congress will add to Medicare by providing new protection against catastrophic acute-care expenses. The new coverage will be financed through a combination of monthly premium increases and a tax liability surcharge on senior citizens. This is a worthwhile improvement that will safeguard older Americans from some devastatingly large health bills. However, we should realize that the premium increases that are slated to finance this new coverage will do almost nothing to remedy the underlying financial imbalances in the existing Medicare system. And if those added premiums fail to keep pace with the cost of the new extra coverage, the imbalances will loom even larger.

It is important to note the difference between the financing sources that are used to pay for the new Medicare protection and the major financing source that we have proposed for meeting the cost of our commitments. The Medicare catastrophic illness protection will be paid for by a flat increase in premiums that all recipients will pay and a surcharge on the tax liability of senior citizens. Our major financing source is neither a premium nor an income tax surcharge; it is a policy decision that an important source of income that was previously exempt from taxation will now no longer be exempt. Thus, what we recommend is a broadening of the base of taxation, as opposed to an increase in the rate of taxation.

The central challenge in Medicare is to devise ways of bringing expected outlays and revenues into line with each other through a combination of cost-control measures, premium increases, and tax increases. Health-cost management techniques put in place in recent years, such as the prospective payment system for hospital reimbursement, will continue to help. But most experts do not expect that

Figure 5.1 Current and Projected Balances in the OASDI and the HI Trust Funds

OASDI Fund Balances

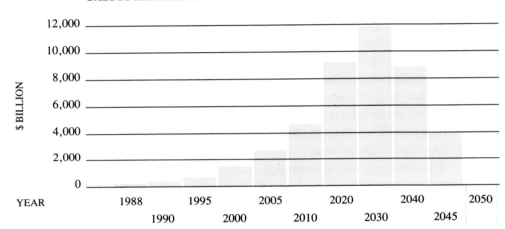

Source: 1988 Annual Report of the Board of Trustees of the Federal Old Age and Survivors' Insurance and Disability Insurance Trust Fund, Table G-1.

HI Fund Balances

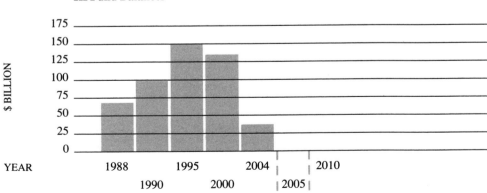

Source: 1988 Annual Report of the Trustees of the Federal Hospital Insurance Trust Fund, Table 11.

such cost-control measures will avoid the painful choices between raising taxes and increasing the financial contributions that the elderly make to Medicare. The situation is made more difficult by the fact that Medicare is headed for trouble even though it hardly addresses one of the most important and rapidly growing needs—long-term care for chronic illness. Consequently, it seems likely that Medicare is going to require both new cost-control measures and new money so the program can assure actuarial soundness in the Hospital Insurance trust fund and extend a greater measure of government protection for long-term care.

Although cost-containment policies are in place for hospitals, Medicare needs a new system of paying individual physicians in order to help bring their cost increases under control. The current system underwrites cost escalation and fails to create incentives for physicians to economize on the use of health services. Other measures might include a greater emphasis on alternative health-care delivery systems and greater government efforts to steer Medicare patients toward "preferred providers" who charge reasonable fees and have demonstrated their cost-effectiveness. These reforms are easier to outline than to implement. One should not underestimate the difficulty of decelerating Medicare cost increases without jeopardizing the quality of health care or access to it.

Creating Protection for Long-Term Care

Even though our society spends about $100 billion per year on Medicare and about $50 billion on Medicaid, the elderly remain vulnerable to the costs of lingering illnesses and disabilities. These costs can be huge ($20,000 to $30,000 annually for nursing home care), and they remain largely outside the social-insurance model of protection.

Aggregate statistics suggest some of the financial problems (but not the emotional strains) that many Americans are going through to help chronically ill spouses and other relatives. Of the $38.1 billion spent for nursing home care in the United States in 1986, only 1.6 percent (or $600 million) was paid for through Medicare and only 0.8 percent (or $300 million) was financed by private health insurance. Thus, less than 3 percent of the total nursing home bill in 1986 was covered by any insurance system. Direct payments by patients and their families accounted for 51 percent of the total, and Medicaid, the means-tested welfare program for health care, paid 41 percent. (The remaining 5 percent of nursing home spending was accounted for by private charity and other government programs.)

The U.S. health-care system is drastically imbalanced in dealing with long-term care. Many of the long-term-care needs of older people are more social than medical in nature; they involve lingering disability rather than disease, are enduring or degenerative rather than episodic or traumatic, and are largely outside the purview of doctors and hospitals. Yet health-care financing for the elderly is still designed for the traditional physician-directed, medical model of hospital care and short-term episodes of acute illness.

The insurance system is also quite fragmented. Care of the elderly calls for an integrated approach to acute and chronic needs. In fact, in some cases a properly managed acute-care system can help avoid the need for long-term care to the extent that it emphasizes prevention, recovery, and independence for patients who have had acute-care episodes. At present, however, reimbursement systems for hospitals and doctors are separate from and poorly coordinated with reimbursement systems for home-care attendants, medical-equipment suppliers, and nursing homes. The public system of reimbursement is not well coordinated with the private voluntary network that provides services such as meals-on-wheels, companionship, and transportation for the elderly.

The result is a regrettable mismatch between needs and services. The most complex, heroic, and often hopeless medical procedures to prolong life are routinely covered, while preventive care, long-term help for chronic disability, rehabilitation, and health education are often neglected. Expensive institutional care is heavily reimbursed, but many home and community-based services are not well covered. Some middle- and upper-middle-income people with minor medical needs pay little for their care, since they are well covered for these routine problems by the combination of Medicare and private "Medigap" insurance. Others who are financially comfortable may suddenly be reduced to poverty should they require long-term care that falls outside the public and private insurance systems. Although the very rich can afford their services and the very poor are covered by Medicaid, all others in need of long-term care are thrown back on their own resources. Once they have "spent down" and become completely destitute, a welfare program in the form of Medicaid comes to the rescue on condition that they enter or remain in a nursing home.

The gap between changing needs and the traditional insurance system will become even larger as our population ages. Today, about 3 million people, or a little over 1 percent of the population, are eighty-five years of age or older. In the coming decades this figure is projected to continue growing to at least 16 million people, or 5 percent of the population, by the middle of the next century. Since we know that the need for assistance with the activities of daily living rises sharply with advancing age, demographics demand that we find ways to finance long-term care efficiently and fairly.

There is something fundamentally wrong with a system in which people must impoverish themselves to find even minimally decent care in their final years. People disagree about how much the government, as opposed to the private sector, should be involved in a new insurance-based approach to financing long-term care. This question is important, but in our view, **the critical issue is to move toward an insurance-based model—whatever the combination of public and private insurance—instead of the present system that relies so heavily on asset depletion and welfare.**

The three major sectors of social protection—the private insurance industry, government insurance programs, and the voluntary sector—must all participate actively in solving the long-term-care problem. **We recommend the use of public subsidies to encourage the spread of private long-term-care insurance,** recognizing that without government participation many people will necessarily be left uncovered and in jeopardy. These subsidies should be national in scope, although this expanded role for the Federal government does not rule out state government involvement.

Government's role could take the form of Medicare coverage for long-term-care expenses after the elderly have incurred a certain amount of out-of-pocket costs. This approach should be supplemented by government subsidies for the purchase of private long-term-care insurance by lower-income households. In this way, government would help people insure themselves against the front-end expenses associated with long-term care, and would provide public coverage for the bigger costs of extended care.

Although some might prefer that the government provide full insurance coverage for long-term care through Part C of Medicare, such a program appears beyond our Federal budget constraints at this time. A more targeted approach to government involvement is appropriate. In particular, we recommend:

- **encouraging private insurance for long-term care, by means of labor-management efforts to integrate such insurance into a flexible benefit package, as well as targeted subsidies (as described above) to help lower-income people purchase private insurance;**

- **educating the public about the need for long-term-care protection;**

- **greater coordination of acute- and long-term-care benefits,** using savings from a better-managed acute-care system—with less unnecessary care—to help finance an extension of long-term-care coverage;

- **greater public and private insurance coverage for home care;**

- **better organization and use of the private nonprofit sector to provide coordinated services to the elderly,** since many of the types of services they need (transportation, delivered meals, counseling) are not normally provided by an insurance-based system;

- **respite care sponsored by community organizations** to relieve spouses and children who care for disabled people; business can also help by arranging for counseling and some flexibility in work time for employees who are also care givers.

The Price Tag

The package of cash-assistance reforms proposed here would cost about $2.6 billion in new spending in the first year. This total is heavily dominated by the proposed increase in ssi benefits. The estimate of $2.5 billion for this new step represents the cost of closing about one-half of the gap between the Federal poverty line and the current level of ssi benefits. It would be possible to recommend a larger increase that would close the gap completely. However, as we noted in our discussion of expanding benefits for children, it is important to recognize fiscal constraints and the need to meet our long-term goals in stages. It is worth noting that the additional $0.1 billion recommended for easing the ssi asset test would permit more than a doubling of the very low asset limits that now screen many low-income senior citizens out of ssi.

Estimates of the cost of greater government involvement in long-term care for the elderly are highly sensitive to assumptions about several program parameters. For example, adding long-term-care coverage to Medicare will cost much more if the coverage becomes available immediately, considerably less if the elderly must spend their own resources for a substantial period of time before qualifying. Obviously, the greater the degree of asset protection under a public program, the greater the government cost. The cost estimate provided here—about $7 billion—is that of a program with a three-year waiting period. This estimate also includes a small amount of funding to begin a program that helps lower-income people purchase private long-term-care insurance. If the waiting period were reduced to two years, the cost would rise to about $15 billion. A program with a rather short waiting period of a few months would cost from $30 billion to $40 billion.

Other factors that affect the cost estimates include whether home care is included in the benefit package, the coinsurance rate (the proportion of costs paid by patients and their families), and the provider payment rates (nursing home reimbursement rates). Costs can be held down, for example, by raising the coinsurance rate or lowering payments to providers. But such steps, if carried too far, could defeat the program's goals. A universal entitlement program for long-term care with a short or no waiting period, low coinsurance rates, and full coverage for home and institutional care might cost the government from $30 billion to $40 billion in the first year, in 1987 dollars. New government spending on that scale isn't likely, given the existing deficit.

Figure 5.2 Projected Costs of Reforms in Programs for the Elderly

Program Initiative	Outlay Increase
Raise ssi benefits	$2.5 billion
Ease ssi asset test	0.1 billion
Subsidize long-term care	7.2 billion
Total	$9.8 billion

A more realistic program would involve either a two- or a three-year waiting period for Federal coverage, coinsurance rates on the order of 30 percent, and a standard that specifies the degree of disability that is required for eligibility. People would be expected to obtain private insurance to help them cover expenses during the waiting period, but the government would subsidize a portion of the premium on a sliding-scale basis for those who cannot afford it. Under such an arrangement, Medicare benefits would begin where the private coverage ends. The difficulty of setting and maintaining a standard of disability for coverage, however, should not be underestimated.

In addition to the net increase of about $7 billion in government outlays, there would also be a big change in the mix of government spending, from the Federal-state sharing of costs that occurs today under Medicaid to a largely Federal-only spending approach under the new program. This would open up some interesting possibilities of tradeoffs: States could take over some of the funding from the Federal government in areas such as economic development in return for the Federal government's expanded role in long-term care.

Chapter Six

In twenty years, social welfare policy in America has passed from soaring confidence to doubt and retrenchment. There has also been a lot of partisan bickering and ideological warfare. The time has come to rise above this partisanship and to tackle our problems head-on. If all the recommendations in this report were implemented, the annual increase in government costs would be about $29 billion. This includes the recommendations for children involving Head Start, WIC, and Medicaid expansion; more funding for drug treatment; the minimum welfare benefit requirement; expanding the Earned Income Tax Credit; new job-training outlays; a public-sector jobs program; and a package of increases to help senior citizens. About one-third of this amount would be allocated to raising SSI benefits and introducing a modest long-term-care program. Since it would be possible to phase in both these new initiatives over time, we could make great progress toward the goals developed in this report with new government outlays in the range of $10 billion to $15 billion per year, phased in during the 1989–92 period and allowing time for our other recommendations to be phased in over a period of several years.

One caveat should be noted. These cost figures are our best estimates of the initial cost to the Federal government when the new initiatives are fully phased in. We have seen a number of instances in which such initial projections turned out to underestimate the eventual cost of the effort. Some factors that inflate costs, such as poor management, are within our control. Others—such as the increased demand for social services that arises when new government coverage draws additional people into a social program—are more difficult to control. What we have done in this report is to make as accurate an estimate as possible of the initial cost of the social investments we propose.

Financing Mechanisms

It is reasonable and fair to ask that those who are financially able help share the cost of social reform. The best way to do that would be to tax Social Security benefits more completely. We believe that approach to be preferable to turning Social Security into a means-tested program. While means-testing might target benefits to those most in need, it would also convert Social Security from the basic pillar of our social insurance system into a welfare program, a socially divisive step.

Beginning in 1984 a portion of Social Security benefits was included in taxable income for the first time. Under present law, one-half of the benefits for individuals with adjusted gross incomes that exceed $25,000 ($32,000 for couples) is subject to income tax, with the proceeds earmarked for the Social Security trust fund. Roughly 10 percent to 15 percent of the elderly now pay taxes on their benefits, and if the income thresholds remain constant over the years, the proportion of people who pay this tax will grow. Lowering the thresholds or eliminating them would bring in more revenue.

An equitable way to expand such taxation would be to tax Social Security benefits rather than freeze or cut cost-of-living adjustments in benefits. This would shield lower-income people from a greater burden while raising substantial amounts of revenue from the higher-income elderly. **Thus we recommend the complete taxation of Social Security benefits that exceed lifetime contributions, using the additional revenues to finance increases in Federal assistance to needy people of all ages.** For example, if a worker contributed $100,000 to Social Security during his or her lifetime, any benefits received in excess of that amount would be reported as taxable income. With this approach, approximately 85 percent of Social Security benefits would be taxed, yielding a total of about $97 billion in Federal revenue over the next five years. We believe that taxing Social Security more completely is preferable to freezing or limiting cost-of-living adjustments in Social Security benefits. Limits on cost-of-living adjustments would apply equally to the elderly widow living on a fixed income and to a wealthy couple. This is clearly unfair.

The actual flow of funds from such additional tax revenues to the needy could be accomplished in more than one way. The important requirement in any such plan is that new outlays must be fully financed in a way that produces no net increase in the Federal government's borrowing requirement.

The revenues collected through additional taxation of Social Security benefits could flow into the Old Age and Survivors' Insurance (OASI) trust fund. A preferable approach, however, would be for the government to establish a special new trust fund earmarked for meeting all the needs identified in this report, including all phases of the life cycle. Such a trust fund could receive additional revenue from the increased taxation of Social Security benefits. The fund could also receive revenues from other sources if the new tax treatment of Social Security does not provide sufficient funding. Increased taxation of Social Security benefits would also increase state tax revenues, which might also be targeted to meet the range of social needs identified in this report.

If a decision were made that it is unwise to divert the money raised by taxing Social Security benefits from the OASI trust fund, it would still be possible to achieve the goal of financing a significant part of our broad agenda of social reform through the greater taxation of Social Security benefits. One approach is to direct the added tax revenues to the OASI fund, while earmarking a portion of the 1990 increase in the payroll tax to address our unmet social needs. The theory behind this is that with the trust fund surplus bolstered by new revenue from taxing benefits, we could afford *not* to put a portion of increased payroll taxes into the trust fund. With this approach, current Social Security recipients might view the taxation of their benefits as a fair way of allocating funds to meet the needs of the elderly poor, while the broader social needs would be paid for by workers' contributions to the payroll tax. A drawback of this approach is that it uses the payroll tax to redistribute income, and that is not one of its major goals. Another approach would place the Supplemental Security Income (SSI) program into the Social Security trust fund, freeing up general revenue in the amount of SSI outlays.

Our preferred approach—setting up a special fund—would reinforce the idea that America is one society with a variety of unmet needs, a place where each group has a stake in what happens to all others. The children and workers of today are also the elderly of tomorrow, and elderly Americans have an immense concern for the well-being of their own and the nation's children and grandchildren. A fund that gives concrete expression to that idea would help counter the divisive "we" versus "they" mentality in social welfare policy.

The Congressional Budget Office has estimated that the additional tax revenue from taxing Social Security as we propose would be $97 billion over the 1989-93 period. Although this would amount to about $19 billion per year if it is spread evenly over the five years, in actuality the revenue gain would start at smaller amounts and grow to nearly $26 billion per year in the latter part of this period. As indicated above, we estimate the full cost of our agenda to the Federal government to be about $29 billion annually when all the program changes are phased in. This figure, however, is a current one, and by 1994 the cost of meeting our agenda would be higher.

It is likely that by the end of five years the annual revenue gain from our proposal would be enough to meet a significant part of the cost of our full agenda. Moreover, as we have stressed in this chapter, some of the more expensive recommendations could be phased in gradually. Indeed, the full taxation of Social Security benefits could also be phased in to smooth the transition for current beneficiaries. The point is that it is possible to implement our recommendations in such a way as to coordinate the required new Federal outlays with the expected revenue gains from the additional Social Security taxation.

A cautionary note should be sounded with respect to the unacceptably high Federal budget deficit. Under a business-as-usual scenario, the Federal deficit, even with the benefit of including the growing Social Security surplus, and assuming no recession and no new programs, will be edging downward only slightly during the next several years, reaching a projected level of $129 billion a year in 1993. If one believes, as we do, that any Social Security surplus should reflect real national saving to be used to meet our obligations to future retirees, and that our targets for reducing the deficit should be geared to the non-Social Security budget, the problem of the deficit is much more serious. In fact, the gap between these two concepts of the deficit—one that includes Social Security and one that excludes it—is likely to grow, reaching about $100 billion in about five years. The projected deficit in 1993, if one excludes the Social Security surplus, is about $220-230 billion; with Social Security the deficit is $129 billion.

In this climate, it is reasonable to expect that many will want to use any new source of revenues to reduce the Federal deficit instead of financing unmet social needs. There is also a danger that if a special fund is set up to meet social needs, the government would cut back what it was already spending on those problems, leaving no net gain. These kinds of pressures face any attempt to move ahead on social problems. In this report we have emphasized both the need to bring the Federal deficit under control and the need to make some additional outlays for much-needed social programs.

Our charge is not to devise a detailed plan for reducing the deficit by proposing expenditure and revenue options. Others with more expertise can do this better than we can. We recognize, however, that the enormity of the Federal deficit will complicate our effort to link any new revenue source with a social agenda that requires a corresponding amount of new government outlays. Ultimately, we need a combination of expenditure and revenue measures that will enable us to capitalize on new targets of opportunity by making prudent increases in government outlays even as we take the tough steps that are necessary to reduce the deficit. We would also like to stress that there are other ways to finance the agenda we have developed. While we strongly prefer the more complete taxation of Social Security benefits, our recommendations should not stand or fall on this preference.

Other options include increases in personal income or corporate tax rates, increases in excise or estate taxes, greater taxation of employee benefits, raising the payroll tax base, and expenditure cuts in program areas ranging from national defense to a host of non-means-tested entitlement and discretionary programs. Of course, it would be possible to combine these categories of options into one financing package. These sources could also be used to make up any shortfall in revenue if our preferred option does not generate enough revenue to meet the actual cost of our recommendations.

Those who are directly responsible to the voters are best equipped to determine the combination of choices that will command the support of a broad cross-section of our people. While no one wants increased taxes or reduced benefits, most Americans also subscribe to the view that a good nation is a caring one.

Chapter Seven

Policy analysts may find it useful to divide a society's problems into their component parts, but the exercise is misleading. When we dwell separately upon the problems of infancy and early childhood, adolescence and young adulthood, older adults, and the aged, we risk obscuring a larger point: the extent to which all the groups of any society are interconnected. However compelling the special needs of each distinct group, each also remains dependent upon the welfare of the others.

The elderly are not alone in their passionate interest in social programs that help with the costs of long-term care. Working adults share this concern, for without such help, the destitute aged may impose crushing financial burdens on their sons and daughters. Similarly, if we rescue young children, even before birth, from the blighting effects of poor nutrition and medical care, not only is their suffering diminished but society saves billions of dollars in future medical costs. The benefits of education are equally profound. America's competitiveness in the world economy, as well as its internal tranquility, depend heavily upon our ability to produce a skilled, well-educated work force, rather than relegating more and more of our young people to an alienated, unproductive underclass.

The continued neglect of these and other social problems threatens to deepen the current conflicts in American society, for the forces of division do not stand still. Most Americans still live in the traditional nuclear family, with two parents to share in producing income, caring for children, and maintaining the home. But more and more families are headed by single parents who find it much harder to cope. In an economy that demands more and more highly skilled workers, those who are well educated can count on commensurate rewards and those who are not so prepared will be able to count on less and less.

We cannot overstate the shortsightedness of ignoring America's social challenges. Granted that not all previous attempts to address them have met with success, and that huge Federal budget deficits discourage new program initiatives. However, these difficulties hardly argue for inaction. Some previous attempts have in fact succeeded, and much has been learned from those that have failed. Some new initiatives could provide help without requiring massive new public expenditures, while others could invest new public funds in the wholly reasonable expectation of a greater return in labor productivity, new tax revenues, and reduced costs.

The panel believes that the American people will accept new social welfare initiatives to the extent that such initiatives respect broadly shared values and have a reasonable prospect of success. We believe that any new approaches to social welfare policy ought to rest on the following principles:

The first is pragmatism. Although the public rightly expresses impatience with social programs that misapply resources or promise more than they can deliver, there is every reason to believe popular support could be generated for those that address obvious problems in a cost-effective way. Programs of prenatal care and early childhood nutrition and development, for example, have been shown to be sound investments that yield vast dividends by averting the costs associated with stunted physical, emotional, and intellectual growth. Business partnerships with high schools have proven effective in expanding school resources and improving student performance. There is a widely felt need for all Americans to be covered by some form of health insurance, and there are workable ideas for a fair sharing of the cost. Similarly, there is broad, often painful, recognition that it makes no sense to continue financing long-term care by forcing certain families to deplete their assets and go on welfare, when equitable, insurance-based programs can be created.

The second principle essential to the acceptance of a new social welfare agenda is respect for the family. For the vast majority of Americans, the family plays the most important role in nurturing individual growth and protecting people in times of adversity. Many of today's most urgent social problems are the direct result of family breakdown. Government policy should strengthen the family rather than undermine it. In this light, programs that help young children are of particular value. They can help prepare children for responsible parental roles. There is also a need for programs that retrain displaced workers and programs that offer direct financial support and do not condition benefits on the absence of a spouse in the home.

The third principle is individual accountability. Social policy should offer protection as well as opportunity, but it ought not to offer the protection in such a way that it fosters dependency and closes off opportunity. For example, programs of aid to unemployed parents ought to condition the benefits on the parents' willingness to pursue job training or education.

A Summary of the Panel's Recommendations

Recognizing these principles, the panel offers the following specific recommendations for each stage of the life cycle. We have made it clear in this report that both the public and private sectors will have to devote some new resources in order to achieve the objectives we have proposed. We have also tried to acknowledge the difficulty of some of the problems we seek to solve. To pay the Federal government's cost of fulfilling our recommendations—a figure the panel estimates at $29 billion a year—we believe that Social Security benefits should be given the same Federal tax treatment as private pensions. Comparable taxation of Social Security and private pension benefits would help raise more than half of the revenues that are required to finance the panel's program of assistance to needy people of all ages. There is no lack of sound ideas. All that is needed is the political will.

Stage 1 – To improve the lives of infants and young children in impoverished homes

- The Federal government should fully fund the WIC program as an entitlement for nutritionally at-risk women and children with incomes up to 185 percent of the Federal poverty line. At the same time, administrators must find ways to improve the management of WIC benefits.

- The government should commit itself to the goal of giving all pregnant women access to prenatal care and well-baby care. Breathing life into this goal will require an outreach effort aimed at people who need these services. It will also involve offering incentives that encourage primary-care physicians such as internists, pediatricians, and obstetricians to serve indigent patients and to provide preventive care.

- The Head Start program should be expanded to increase the number of slots so that many more of the eligible three- and four-year-olds can participate. More of these slots should be for full-day programs for children with working parents. Very low-income parents, especially teenage mothers with children below age three, should receive expanded family support, referral, and home visiting services. Staff of early childhood development programs should receive better compensation and training.

- Adequate Federal funding should also be provided for other measures that benefit children, including Social Services Block Grants, AFDC-Foster Care, the Child Abuse Prevention and Treatment Act, the child welfare services provisions of the Social Security Act, and continued research on child welfare problems at the National Institute of Child Health and Human Development. It is also important to provide financial and informational support to states and localities that seek to improve services for young children.

- The Federal government should subsidize lower-income families by refunding an amount equal to the existing tax credit for day-care services to families whose incomes are too low to permit taking a credit.

- States and localities should test and implement new approaches to providing family-support services that feature effective early intervention, parent education, and the coordination of diverse public programs.

Stage 2 – To ease the transition from school to work for poor adolescents and young adults

- The panel endorses the pursuit of business partnerships with schools to enhance school resources.

- The panel endorses ongoing efforts to prevent teenagers from becoming pregnant and to provide counseling, health services, and day care for those who do.

- The panel calls for treatment on demand for all drug users who seek help.

- The Congress should maintain or restore adequate funding for programs aimed at disadvantaged adolescents, including the Job Training Partnership Act, the Job Corps, the Summer Youth Employment Program, and Chapter 1 of the Education Consolidation and Improvement Act.

- State governors and legislatures should use their power to direct Federal funds to leverage local action in a concerted, sustained attack on the problems of young people who are at risk of failing to make the school-to-work transition. There should be interagency state youth councils composed of senior officials from education, job-training, and human-services agencies. The councils should be charged with coordinating service delivery, sharing information, and maintaining continuity and quality control in local programs for at-risk youth.

■ Every community should consider establishing a committee composed of school, job-training, and business representatives, to be charged with assessing the state of local youth resources and developing a plan to deal with deficiencies. Such committees ought to bear in mind:

> the usefulness of schools as centers for delivering integrated services to adolescents;

> the need for early detection to forestall problems;

> the interrelatedness of leaving school, teenage parenthood, unemployment, and welfare dependency;

> the need to offer young people personal reasons to succeed in life and work;

> the importance of private-sector involvement.

Stage 3 – To enhance opportunities and secure protections for Americans of working age

■ The Federal budget deficit should be reduced in steps that achieve real long-term savings. These may include reductions in entitlement benefits, discretionary non-defense programs, and non-critical national defense outlays. They may also include tax increases.

■ The Federal government should do what it can to arrest the decline in savings and to increase private investment.

■ Business and labor should encourage flexible compensation, incentive pay, and profit-sharing arrangements, along with changes in obsolete management practices and work rules. Other desirable measures should enable workers to change jobs without losing pension and health benefits.

■ The purchasing power of the minimum wage should be returned to its 1981 level.

■ The earned income tax credit should be expanded by varying its benefits with the size of the recipient's family.

■ The Federal government should require employers either to offer a basic package of health insurance coverage to workers or to contribute an amount per employee to a fund that will finance coverage for uninsured workers.

■ Medicaid should be reformed in the following ways:

> Coverage should be assured to the poor who do not qualify for employer-mandated coverage.

> Coverage should not be limited to those receiving cash welfare assistance.

> The program should place more emphasis on early treatment and preventive health care.

■ Unemployment Insurance should be reformed in these ways:

> Administration of the program ought to be tightened up, especially by requiring claimants to make more serious efforts to seek work.

> Unemployed persons in declining labor markets should be able to receive their benefits as lump-sum payments that can be used to move to a more promising labor market.

> The schedule of UI benefits should be recast so that they are high for the first several weeks, and then decline gradually as more training and employment services are provided. Benefits for those who have experienced a long period of unemployment should be extended beyond the normal termination period only if the recipient agrees to participate in a serious retraining program.

Solvency standards should be established to put the state unemployment systems on a sounder and more equal financial footing. In addition, differences in benefit levels between states should be narrowed by increasing benefits in states where they are particularly low.

In regard to AFDC:

By the 1990s the Federal government should establish a national minimum benefit standard (AFDC plus food stamps) equal to two-thirds of the Federal poverty level.

The welfare system ought to emphasize work instead of long-term dependency, especially by setting a limit on the length of time those who are capable of working may receive welfare benefits. Such a limit would be coupled with the provision of a public-sector job for those who have exhausted their benefits but cannot find work.

Stage 4 – To enhance protection of the aged and their families

- The government should increase Federal SSI benefits to assure decent income for all the elderly, ease restrictive limits on liquid assets in order to qualify for SSI, and conduct outreach programs to increase the participation of those eligible for SSI.

- The government should save and invest the surpluses building up in the Social Security trust funds, instead of spending them for consumption of current services.

- Regarding long-term care:

    The critical issue is to move toward an insurance-based model, whatever the combination of public and private insurance. Public subsidies could encourage such a move, as could labor-management efforts to integrate such insurance into a flexible benefit package.

    Families and individuals should not have to pauperize themselves in order to become eligible for public long-term-care benefits.

The public must be educated about each individual's need for long-term-care insurance.

Acute- and long-term-care benefits should be better coordinated.

There is a need for greater public and private insurance for home care.

With better organization, the private nonprofit sector could provide better coordinated services to the elderly.

Community organizations might provide more respite care to the families of those who are caring for the disabled elderly.

Appendix A

Notes and Sources

The major sources used in developing the analysis and recommendations contained in this report are listed under each chapter head. In addition, the following sources were used in calculating the figures on income, demographics, benefits, program expenditures, and new revenue outlays cited throughout the report:

Bureau of the Census, Current Population Survey (CPS), *Money Income of Families, Households and Persons in the United States: 1987,* and *Characteristics of the Population Below the Poverty Line* (August 1988).

Committee on Ways and Means, U.S. House of Representatives, *Background Material and Data on Programs Within the Jurisdiction of the Committee on Ways and Means* (March 1988).

Congressional Budget Office, *Reducing the Deficit: Spending and Revenue Options, A Report to the Senate and House Committees on the Budget* (Annual Report, March 1989).

Chapter One–Reexamining Our Social Welfare System

Bernstein, Merton, and Joan Bernstein, *Social Security* (New York: Basic Books, 1988).

Cherlin, Andrew (ed.), *The Changing American Family and Public Policy* (Washington, D.C.: Urban Institute Press, 1988).

Ellwood, David, *Divide and Conquer,* Occasional Paper 1, Ford Foundation Project on Social Welfare and the American Future (New York: Ford Foundation, 1987).

Gueron, Judith, *Reforming Welfare with Work,* Occasional Paper 2, Ford Foundation Project on Social Welfare and the American Future (New York: Ford Foundation, 1987).

Harris, Louis, *Inside America* (New York: Random House, 1987).

93

Levy, Frank, *Dollars and Dreams: The Changing American Income Distribution*. The Population of the U.S. in the 1980s: A Census Monograph Series (New York: Russell Sage Foundation, 1987).

Melville, Keith, and John Doble, *The Public's Perspective on Social Welfare Reform* (New York: Public Agenda Foundation, 1988).

Minarik, Joseph, "Family Incomes," in Isabel V. Sawhill (ed.), *Challenge to Leadership: Economic and Social Issues for the Next Decade* (Washington, D.C.: Urban Institute Press, 1988).

Quinn, Joseph, "The Economic Status of the Elderly," *Review of Income and Wealth,* March 1987.

Schorr, Lisbeth B., *Within Our Reach: Breaking the Cycle of Disadvantage* (New York: Anchor/Doubleday, 1988).

Wilson, William J., *The Truly Disadvantaged: The Inner City Underclass and Public Policy* (Chicago: University of Chicago Press, 1987).

Chapter Two–Infancy and Childhood: A Time to Sow

Berreuta-Clement, John R., et al., *Changed Lives: The Effects of the Perry Preschool Program on Youths Through Age 19* (Ypsilanti, Mich.: High/Scope Educational Research Foundation, 1984).

Centers for Disease Control, *U.S. Immunization Survey* (1987).

Children's Defense Fund, *A Children's Defense Budget Fiscal Year 1989: An Analysis of Our Nation's Investment in Children* (Washington, D.C.: Children's Defense Fund, 1988).

Chollet, Deborah, *Uninsured in the U.S.: The Nonelderly Population Without Health Insurance, 1986* (Washington, D.C.: Employee Benefits Research Institute, 1988).

Congressional Budget Office, *Reducing Poverty Among Children* (Washington, D.C.: U.S. Government Printing Office, 1985).

Deutsch, Martin, Theresa Jordan, and Cynthia Deutsch, "Long-Term Effects of Early Intervention," Institute for Developmental Studies Paper (New York: New York University, 1985).

Ellwood, *Divide and Conquer, op. cit.*

Friedman, Dana, "Corporate Financial Assistance for Child Care" (New York: The Conference Board, 1985).

Garfinkel, Irwin, and Sara S. McLanahan, *Single Mothers and Their Children* (Washington, D.C.: Urban Institute Press, 1986).

Gershenson, Charles, Center for the Study of Social Policy, Office of Children and Youth of the Department of Health Services. Private interview.

Harvey, Stefan, Robert Greenstein, and Scott Barancik, *Saving to Serve More: Ways to Reduce WIC Infant Formula Costs* (Washington, D.C.: Center on Budget and Policy Priorities, 1988).

Hayes, Cheryl D. (ed.), *Risking the Future* (Washington, D.C.: National Academy Press, 1987).

Institute of Medicine, *Preventing Low Birthweight* (Washington, D.C.: National Academy Press, 1985).

Kahn, Alfred J., and Sheila B. Kamerman, *Child Care: Facing the Hard Choices* (Dover, Mass.: Auburn House, 1987).

Reisman, Barbara J., Amy J. Moore, and Karen Fitzgerald, *Child Care: The Bottom Line* (New York: Child Care Action Campaign, 1988).

Weikart, David P., *Quality Preschool Programs: A Long-Term Social Investment*, Occasional Paper 5, Ford Foundation Project on Social Welfare and the American Future (New York: Ford Foundation, 1989).

Weikart, David P., Lawrence Schweinhart, and Jeffrey Koshel, "Policy Options for Preschool Programs" (Ypsilanti, Mich.: High/Scope Early Childhood Policy Papers, 1986).

Chapter Three–Young Adulthood: Preparing for a World of Work

Berlin, Gordon, and Andrew Sum, *Toward A More Perfect Union,* Occasional Paper 3, Ford Foundation Project on Social Welfare and the American Future (New York: Ford Foundation, 1988).

Danziger, Sandra, "Breaking the Chains: From Teenage Girls to Welfare Mothers or, Can Social Welfare Policy Increase Options?" in Jack A. Meyer (ed.), *Ladders Out of Poverty* (Washington, D.C.: American Horizons Foundation, 1986).

deLone, Richard H., *State Governments and At-Risk Youth: The Critical Link* (Philadelphia: Public/Private Ventures, 1987).

Furstenberg, Frank F., J. Brooks-Gunn, and S. Philip Morgan, *Adolescent Mothers in Later Life* (Cambridge: Cambridge University Press, 1987).

Hahn, Andrew, Jacqueline Danzberger, and Bernard Lefkowitz, *Dropouts in America: Enough Is Known for Action* (Washington, D.C.: Institute for Educational Leadership, 1987).

Hoffertz, S.L., and C.D. Hayes (eds.), *Risking the Future,* v.2 (Washington, D.C.: National Academy Press, 1987).

McMullan, Bernard J., and Phyllis Snyder, *Allies in Education* (Philadelphia: Public/Private Ventures, 1987).

Moore, Kristin A., "Teenage Pregnancy: The Dimensions of the Problem," *New Perspectives* (Summer, 1985).

Moore, Kristin A., M.C. Simms, and C.L. Betsey, *Choice and Circumstance: Racial Differences in Adolescent Sexuality and Fertility* (Washington, D.C.: Urban Institute Press, 1986).

Parekh, Neeta, Shi-Feng Chuang, and Andrew Sum, "A Profile of Participants in JAG School to Work Transition Programs, Class of 1988" (Boston: Northeastern University Center for Labor Market Studies, October 1988).

Peng, Samuel S., *High School Dropouts: A National Concern* (Washington, D.C.: National Center for Educational Statistics, U.S. Department of Education, Educational Commission of the States, March 1985).

Sipe, Cynthia, Jean Groshan, and Julita A. Milliner, *STEP: Report on the 1986 Experience* (Philadelphia: Public/Private Ventures, 1987).

Smith, Thomas, Gary C. Walker, and Rachel A. Baker, "Youth and the Workplace: Second-Chance Programs and the Hard-to-Serve," paper prepared for the William T. Grant Foundation Commission on Family, Work and Citizenship (Philadelphia: Public/Private Ventures, 1988).

Sum, Andrew, and Robert Taggart with Gordon Berlin, "Cutting Through," paper prepared for the Ford Foundation Project on Social Welfare and the American Future, 1986.

Sum, Andrew, Neal Fogg, and Robert Taggart, "Withered Dreams: The Decline in the Economic Fortunes of Young, Non-College Educated Male Adults and Their Families," paper prepared for the William T. Grant Foundation Commission on Family, Work and Citizenship (Boston: Northeastern University Center for Labor Market Studies, 1988).

Taggart, Robert, *The Comprehensive Competencies Program: A New Way to Teach, A New Way to Learn* (Washington, D.C.: Remediation and Training Institute, 1986).

Chapter Four–The Working Years:
Increasing Economic Opportunity and Social Protection

Blank, Rebecca M., and Alan S. Blinder, "Macroeconomics, Income Distribution and Poverty," in Sheldon H. Danziger and Daniel H. Weinberg (eds.), *Fighting Poverty: What Works and What Doesn't* (Cambridge, Mass.: Harvard University Press, 1986).

Coalition on Human Needs, *How the Poor Would Remedy Poverty* (Washington, D.C.: Coalition on Human Needs, 1988).

Ellwood, *Divide and Conquer, op. cit.*

Ellwood, David, *Poor Support: Poverty in the American Family* (New York: Basic Books, 1988).

Friedman, Barry L., and Robert I. Lerman, "The Role of Employer-Provided Benefits in Achieving Social Protections," paper prepared for a seminar on The Role of Employer Benefits in Future Social Welfare Policy, Heller School, Brandeis University, 1989.

Gueron, *Reforming Welfare with Work, op. cit.*

Gueron, Judith, *Work Initiatives for Welfare Recipients*: *Lessons from a Multi-State Experiment* (New York: Manpower Demonstration Research Corporation, 1986).

Levitan, Sar, and Isaac Shapiro, *Working But Poor: America's Contradictions* (Baltimore: Johns Hopkins University Press, 1987).

Levy, *Dollars and Dreams, op. cit.*

Reischauer, Robert D., testimony before the Subcommittee on Social Security and Family Policy of the Committee on Finance, U.S. Senate, February 23, 1987.

Sawhill, Isabel V., "Poverty and the Underclass," in Sawhill (ed.), *Challenge to Leadership, op. cit.*

Chapter Five–Old Age: A Time to Reap and Sow Again

Andrews, Emily S., *The Changing Profile of Pensions in America* (Washington, D.C.: Employee Benefit Research Institute, 1985).

Bernstein, Merton, and Bernstein, *Social Security, op. cit.*

Palmer, John, "Financing Health Care and Retirement for the Aged," in Sawhill (ed.), *Challenge to Leadership, op. cit.*

Weiner, Joshua, and David Kennell, "Catastrophic Long-Term Care Insurance: A Public/Private Partnership," paper prepared for the U.S. Department of Health and Human Services Task Force on Long-Term Health Care Policies, May 1987.

Zedlewski, Sheila, and Jack A. Meyer, *Toward Alleviating Poverty Among the Elderly and Disabled* (Washington, D.C.: Urban Institute Press, 1987).

Appendix B

Research Funded by the
Ford Foundation Project on Social
Welfare and the American Future

Coalition on Human Needs, Washington, D.C.
"How the Poor Would Remedy Poverty: A Survey"

Fay Cook, Northwestern University
"Convergent Perspectives on Social Welfare Policy: The Views from the General Public, Members of Congress and AFDC Recipients"

Mary Corcoran et al., University of Michigan
"The Intergenerational Transmission of Poverty and Welfare"

Martha Derthick, University of Virginia
"The Plight of the Social Security Administration Since 1970"

David Ellwood, Harvard University
"Social Welfare Reform: A Categorical Perspective"

Tekie Fessehatzion, Jackson State University
"The Effects of Government Public Assistance Programs on the Economic Well-Being of the Mississippi Delta Poor"

Edward Gramlich, University of Michigan
"Local Government and Private Charity Responses to Federal Welfare State Programs"

Russell Hanson, Indiana University
"The Dynamics of Welfare in a Federal System: A View from the States"

Leonard Hausman, Brandeis University
"Employer Benefits and the Future of the Social Protection System"

Hugh Heclo, George Mason University
"The Responsible Society: Taking Stock of American Social Policy"

Bruce Jacobs, University of Rochester
"Media Portrayals, Public Understanding, and Policy Options for U.S. Programs Benefiting the Elderly"

Christopher Jencks, Northwestern University
"An Assessment of Poverty and Hardship in America"

Ira Katznelson, New School for Social Research
"Setting the Social Welfare Policy Agenda"

Robert Lerman, Brandeis University
"Developing a Strategy for Reducing Poverty Outside the Welfare System"

Frank Levy and Richard Michel, Urban Institute, Washington, D.C.
"Economic Growth, Standards of Living, Income Inequality and Related Welfare Needs and Responses"

Michael Lipsky and Stephen R. Smith, Massachusetts Institute of Technology
"Recent Changes in Government/Non-Profit Relations"

Manpower Demonstration Research Corporation, New York, N.Y.
"Work/Welfare Initiatives: Lessons from a Multi-Site Demonstration"

Kay McChesney, University of Southern California
"Homeless Women and Their Children"

Keith Melville and John Doble, Public Agenda Foundation, New York, N.Y.
"Social Welfare Policy, the Public Perspective: Focus Groups and Citizen Review Panels on Reform Proposals"

North Carolina Center for Public Policy Research, Raleigh, N.C.
"Sitting Down Together: Community Forums on Future Aging Policy in North Carolina"

Ann Schnare and Sandra Newman, Urban Institute, Washington, D.C.
"A Reassessment of Shelter Assistance in America"

Robert Shapiro, Columbia University
"Trends in Public Opinion Toward Social Welfare Policy"

Theda Skocpol, Harvard University
"The Politics of Social Provision in the United States"

Timothy Smeeding, Vanderbilt University
"The Luxembourg Income Study Project"

Social Science Research Council, New York, N.Y.
"The New Survey of Income and Program Participation"

Harold Watts, Columbia University
"Family Stability and Economic Well-Being Among Black and
White Children"

Harold L. Wilensky, University of California, Berkeley
"The Political Economy of Welfare in International Perspective"

William J. Wilson, University of Chicago
"Poverty and Family Structure in the Inner City"

Research Advisory Committee

Hugh Heclo, George Mason University, *Chair*

Fay L. Cook, Northwestern University

Edward M. Gramlich, University of Michigan

Ira Katznelson, New School for Social Research

Alicia Munnell, Federal Reserve Bank of Boston

William J. Wilson, University of Chicago

Appendix C

Occasional Papers of the
Ford Foundation Project on Social
Welfare and the American Future

1. David T. Ellwood, *Divide and Conquer: Responsible Security for America's Poor* (1987).

2. Judith M. Gueron, *Reforming Welfare with Work* (1987).

3. Gordon Berlin and Andrew Sum, *Toward A More Perfect Union: Basic Skills, Poor Families, and Our Economic Future* (1988).

4. Lawrence D. Brown, *Health Policy in the United States: Issues and Options* (1988).

5. David P. Weikart, *Quality Preschool Programs: A Long-Term Social Investment* (1989).

6. Frank Levy, *Poverty and Economic Growth* (forthcoming).